SUCCESSFUL ACQUISITION OF UNQUOTED COMPANIES

Third Edition

To Gavin . . . a natural leader

SUCCESSFUL ACQUISITION OF UNQUOTED COMPANIES

A Practical Guide

Third Edition

Barrie Pearson
of Livingstone Fisher Associates Plc

Gower

in association with
The Chartered Institute of
Management Accountants

First published 1983

Second edition 1986

Third edition published 1989 by
Gower Publishing Company Limited
Gower House,
Croft Road,
Aldershot
Hants GU11 3HR,
England

Gower Publishing Company,
Old Post Road,
Brookfield,
Vermont 05036,
U.S.A.

British Library Cataloguing in Publication Data

Pearson, Barrie
    Successful acquisition of unquoted companies —
    3rd ed. —
    1. Great Britain.   Unquoted companies.
    Acquisition.   Management aspects.
    I. Title   II. Chartered Institute of
    Management Accountants
    658.1'6

ISBN 0 566 02814 X

Typeset by C. R. Barber & Partners (Highlands) Ltd,
Fort William, Scotland

Printed and bound in Great Britain at
The Camelot Press plc, Southampton

Contents

Preface

Management research has shown that more than one half of acquisitions are less successful than expected. Mistakes are always expensive, and sometimes disastrous. Unquoted acquisitions can be more complex and hazardous than acquiring much larger quoted companies.

The aim of this book is to provide a structured framework and a practical step-by-step guide to help people complete successfully the acquisition of unquoted companies and subsidiaries of quoted ones. Much of the content, however, is applicable to the acquisition of quoted companies. Equally, prospective vendors of both unquoted companies and subsidiaries of quoted ones should find the book helpful in planning their approach.

This third edition contains additional material and current insights on various important aspects of the acquisition process. These include the commercial rationale behind successful acquisitions; improved search techniques to identify attractive acquisition targets; the use of valuation techniques to determine the worth of a company; performance-related purchases, which have become more frequent; how to achieve cost-effective accountants' investigation of a target company; acquiring from a receiver; and successful post-acquisition management. Additionally, a summary of key points is included at the end of each chapter.

The book has been written for those involved in the acquisition process. These include chief executives, directors, entrepreneurs, business development executives and senior managers, as well as the accountants in the companies directly involved. Practising accountants and lawyers will also find this book useful.

The book covers more than the acquisition itself. Successful acquisition begins with a clearly stated commercial strategy and rationale, rather than simply a determination to acquire. And it does not end with the signing of the contract: successful acquisition involves producing the anticipated results from the acquired company and maintaining a highly motivated management team and workforce under new ownership.

Regulations and controls have been excluded from the book. These tend to change frequently, and out-of-date information is dangerous. Up-to-date professional advice from a solicitor or accountant practising in the country concerned is necessary.

A chapter has been added on management buy-outs and buy-ins, because these are an established method for disposing of companies. Equally importantly, however, opportunities are provided for the executive team to have management control of the company and to obtain a valuable equity stake, in return for a modest personal investment.

There is no magic formula to guarantee the acquisition of a company at a realistic price, let alone to ensure success afterwards. The book is simply intended measurably to enhance the chances of success.

Livingstone Fisher Associates Plc   Barrie Pearson
Acre House, 69–76 Long Acre,
London WC2E 9JW

1 Background

Takeover bids of large public companies make front page headlines in the financial press, and sometimes in the popular daily newspapers. The vast majority of acquisitions, however, are of unquoted companies and divisions or subsidiaries of quoted ones. The publicity received may be only a paragraph in an inside page of a financial newspaper, but this does not reduce their corporate significance. It is a fact not always appreciated that there are several thousand private companies in the UK with a turnover exceeding £3 million.

The strategic significance of the acquisition of an unquoted company by a large quoted group may be quite disproportionate to the size of the deal. For example, it may provide a speedy and significant entry, perhaps belatedly, into an attractive and rapidly growing market segment.

In recent years, a number of unquoted companies have developed microprocessor-based building management systems. This is a market with a huge potential, which requires a substantial investment in research and development. Not surprisingly, some large quoted companies have acquired private companies in this sector, because of the difficulty of assembling an experienced development team and the lengthy lead time required to launch a competitive product from scratch.

The key to the success of any acquisition is the ability to accelerate the organic growth achieved under new ownership. Compatibility of the management styles and key people in the two companies is essential. Otherwise some of these key people may leave or switch off, and a 'them' and 'us' conflict may persist for years.

If the management and workforce of the acquired company are able to see tangible benefits in prospect, this provides an excellent starting point to achieve success. For example, a successful company making computerized equipment for the graphic arts industry enjoyed a substantial opportunity as a result of being acquired. Previously exports had been limited by a lack of finance and people. Suddenly the company had access to worldwide distribution and field service networks as a ready-made base from which to expand. The workforce could see the benefits in terms of job prospects, and the acquisition was off to a flying start.

Let us now examine the motivation of both parties and the potential benefits which the acquisition offers each of them.

The Potential Vendor

Quoted groups of companies actively dispose of subsidiaries and divisions which are no longer regarded as part of their core businesses. An unsolicited approach to purchase a subsidiary is likely to be considered dispassionately.

In sharp contrast, some private companies have an unswerving commitment to preserve their independence and emphatically reject any approach whatsoever. Only personal circumstances, such as the death or terminal illness of a key director or substantial shareholder or a major disagreement between the people involved, may prompt a change of attitude towards the subject of acquisition.

Many companies, however, respond more positively for various reasons, for example:

- They are prepared to explore briefly any serious approach.

- If the next generation of the family is not capable of managing the business, or unwilling to do so, then approaching retirement may prompt a sale of the company.

- A common problem of the successful unquoted company wishing to expand is a shortage of funds. The shareholders are often reluctant or unable to provide more equity capital themselves, and borrowings are probably at a realistic limit already. Selling the company, and retaining the management team, may provide a solution.

- When stock market conditions are favourable, there is an opportunity for shareholders to realize some cash and to raise additional funds for the company without losing control. The creation of the Unlisted Securities Market and the Third Market in the United Kingdom have made this possible for many more companies. Nonetheless, some unquoted companies are still hesitant to take such a step and a compatible acquirer may provide a more acceptable answer.

- Some shrewd unquoted companies will recognise that performance has peaked, or is about to, and will set out to sell 'at the top'.

The Bidder

Some companies reject the prospect of approaching unquoted companies because if the shareholders say 'no' emphatically enough, that is the end of the matter. This is true, at least for the time being. However, many successful unquoted acquisitions have resulted from approaches to companies which had not considered selling within the foreseeable future. Potential vendors must be persuaded and cajoled into selling, by being shown the potential benefits for the shareholders, directors and workforce.

There are benefits to bidders acquiring unquoted companies, rather than quoted ones, including:

- Unquoted companies are likely to be purchased at a significant discount to a quoted one in the same industry sector.

- It should be possible to manage the negotiations to avoid a contested bid situation.

- An opportunity to acquire a business with proven, entrepreneurial management.

- The ability to obtain more information about the

prospects for an unquoted company, given willing potential vendors.

- Where growth has been constrained, a significant cash injection for expansion may produce handsome returns.

- Questions of monopolies and fair trading may be avoided because of the smaller size of company involved.

The background issues, having been examined from both sides, now the questions of strategy and commercial rationale need to be considered by the potential bidder as a first step.

2 Strategic Issues

Before even contemplating an acquisition, both public and unquoted companies need to decide their overall strategy and commercial rationale. This demands much more than stating vague aspirations. It requires clear thinking and careful wording. If normal business planning exists in the company or subsidiary, a summary of the plan should be adequate. If not, two sides of paper are all that is needed provided that the analysis and thinking has been sufficiently rigorous. Do not be tempted to short-cut the thinking process, because the consequence could be expensive mistakes later.

The key issues to consider in deciding an effective company strategy include:

- The direction of the company, which requires a vision of its future business.

- The resources available or obtainable.

- The organizational structure and management style appropriate.

To achieve the necessary detail, a number of specific questions should then be answered rigorously:

- Which existing market segments should we concentrate our future effort and investment on? Why? Has the choice been researched adequately?

- Which countries (or regions) should we concentrate on?

- Which market segments or countries/regions do we plan to enter? Have we considered alternatives adequately?

- How will our commercial rationale differentiate us from our competitors?

- Which market segments, countries and products should we phase out of, or withdraw from?

- Which divisions and subsidiaries should we consider selling? Or encouraging management buy-outs?

- What finance, people, and expertise can be made available to achieve our goals? Are these adequate? If not, how can the shortfall be overcome?

- What threats or opportunities may be posed by changes in technology, political factors, legislation, competitors, suppliers, economic factors? What contingency plans are needed?

- Are our organizational structure, management development programmes and staff recruitment programmes designed to help achieve our plans? If not, what changes should be made?

The special considerations required for overseas acquisitions are outlined in a later chapter.

Acquisition Rationale

If the possibility of acquisition features in the business strategy, then the reasons for acquiring a company should be written down as a discipline.

There is always the potential danger that executive ego or personal ambition, coupled with the mistaken belief that big is necessarily beautiful, will become the motivating force leading to acquisition. Some of the largest multinational companies require their subsidiaries to use external acquisition advisers; and an important benefit is their dispassionate approach, free from internal political bias. A written statement of the rationale for acquisition helps guard against an emotive approach.

Sound reasons for acquisition include:

- To achieve market leadership or to increase market share, and so reduce competition — subject, in various countries, to monopolies, fair trading and anti-trust regulations, etc.

- To broaden an existing product range in existing markets and territories.

- To diversify by acquiring the necessary management, marketing and technical expertise to provide a worthwhile market share quickly.

- To enter another region or country, provided

that sufficient research and analysis has been done.

● To penetrate an additional distribution channel or to acquire access to certain major customers.

● To protect a key source of supply which otherwise may be acquired by a competitor.

● To acquire additional resources, such as a factory or distribution network, more quickly than starting from scratch.

● To invest surplus funds from existing operations, provided the commercial rationale is sound and relevant opportunities exist.

More generally, an acquisition may be regarded as valid if it is the most attractive way to achieve previously defined commercial goals. An acid test, however, is to outline the ways in which the target company would be managed and developed more effectively by the acquirer than the present owners.

Two dubious reasons sometimes given for acquisition are to achieve synergy or to snap up a bargain.

Synergy can be quantified easily with a calculator, but the benefits often prove difficult to achieve. Synergy has been described as a case of $2+2=5$. For example, integrating and rationalizing the sales forces of two companies following an acquisition: it is easy to overlook the initial expense and delay involved before any savings will result. Additional costs may come initially from redundancy payments, relocation costs, retraining staff and various other items depending upon the circumstances. Also, the subsequent savings may be less than expected because of unwillingness persisting amongst the people involved.

Buying a company at a bargain price may seem

attractive. There have been cases where a company has been acquired for £1, together with the liabilities involved. Some of these have proved to be most onerous and expensive acquisitions. Companies available at knockdown prices are likely to need drastic surgery. Success is not achieved by eliminating operating losses, which is merely the preliminary step. Success demands that an adequate return on total funds invested is achieved within an acceptable time.

The problems of turning round loss-making companies merit careful consideration. The skills required are very different from those needed to run successful businesses. Executives good at one of these, are often unsuited to the other. So a key issue is to ensure that a team with proven and relevant track records is available immediately a company requiring a turnround is acquired. Chapter 11 is devoted to this subject.

Key Point Summary

- Define the future direction of the company in terms of market segments and territories to concentrate on.

- Write down the specific reasons for acquisition before attempting to identify target companies.

- Install a full-time chief executive from day one, preferably with previous turn-round experience, when acquiring a loss-making company.

3 Alternatives to Acquisition

An outright acquisition should be the last alternative to be considered. It is tempting to think that an acquisition will automatically provide a neat short-cut way to develop the business. Like exporting, acquisitions involve a lot of hard work without any guarantee of success. The alternatives to be considered include:

Organic Growth

When a company has the people available to develop and launch new products, or can recruit staff, or possibly headhunt the nucleus of a team, the funds required could be much less than those needed for an acquisition.

If the market is developing rapidly, or the company has been slow to enter the market, then organic growth may take too long to achieve an acceptable market share. Organic growth cannot be dismissed, however, as efforts to make acquisitions should be more than matched by work on internal business development projects in the company.

Distribution and Manufacturing Agreements

This type of agreement may provide an opportunity to achieve additional profits and cash flow relatively quickly, for a small initial investment. Alternatively, it may be a deliberate first step towards making an acquisition approach to the company within the medium term.

In some industry sectors, this kind of arrangement is widespread. For example branded lagers and soft drinks are produced and bottled under licence in many countries. In high technology industries, such as electronics, the use of local distributors overseas is widespread in order to provide the maintenance and field service support needed.

There are countless opportunities available, however, in industries where this type of arrangement is at present uncommon. Companies wishing to pursue this kind of opportunity have to take the initiative. In the USA, for example, many small and medium-sized companies may have restricted themselves to selling in the home market until now. A British giftware company convinced a US manufacturer that there was a profitable UK market for a patented tableware product. Initially, a UK distribution agreement was negotiated. This proved successful and today the product is manufactured in the UK in a joint venture company.

Some companies are understandably wary of distributing products to be sold under the manufacturer's brand name. There is always the possibility that the distribution agreement may be terminated when sales have been built up, and before an acceptable return has been achieved, and that the manufacturer will then take over the overseas distribution. Rather than reject an opportunity for this reason, agreements should be negotiated which are equitable to both parties. A key feature should be a reasonable length of agreement, and an adequate period of notice required for termination by either party. This provides both sides with the time required to make alternative arrangements.

A Minority Equity Stake

Acquiring a minority equity stake is recommended only in specific circumstances. The danger which must be avoided is being 'locked' into an unlisted company without management control, or even significant influence. In such a case the only available way to realize the investment may be to offer the minority equity stake for purchase by the other shareholders.

A minority stake may be appropriate when purchasing in a country where one has only limited knowledge of the cultural, social and management customs. If a minority stake is acquired for these reasons the purchase should provide:

- Immediate board representation to provide the opportunity to learn more about the business and to influence future development.

- An option to acquire either majority or outright control within a given period and at a prescribed price or valuation formula.

In some countries such as Nigeria, legislation demands that foreign companies are restricted to minority equity stakes in certain industries. Provided management control can be achieved, this may be better than rejecting the opportunity altogether. Another key factor in the decision may be the ability to repatriate funds.

One reason to acquire and retain only a minority stake may be to secure distribution outlets. For example, an insurance company may acquire minority equity stakes in chains of estate agents primarily to capture all of their insurance business with a minimum investment.

Another possible reason for taking a minority stake is to seek some form of preferential treatment from a key supplier. This may be a sound reason, but the trap of investing in a key supplier to avoid the company being wound up could prove to be an expensive way of merely delaying the inevitable loss of a source of supply.

Whenever a minority stake in a supplier is being considered, the commercial rationale should be rigorously examined and alternative sources of supply evaluated before deciding to invest.

A Joint Venture or Consortium

There are numerous cases where the parties involved in a joint venture or consortium have ended up bickering with each other. Consequently, people are rightly wary of the prospect of a joint venture, let alone the thought of a consortium involving three or more partners. In certain situations, however, a joint venture may make sense. For example, where:

- The funds are insufficient to make an acquisition of the appropriate size; or there are no suitable companies to be purchased.

- The degree of risk is too large for the company to undertake alone. Projects of this kind may include oil, gas and mineral exploration.

- An overseas market or project requires a wider range of expertise than the company is able to provide. For example, construction projects requiring specialist underwater work.

If a joint venture or consortium is selected as appropriate for developing the business, then the following aspects will help achieve success:

- Selecting partners with a compatible management style, especially if overseas companies are to participate. If diversification is involved, obtaining complementary skills which will provide the new venture with an adequate breadth of expertise.

- Agreeing at the outset on the management team to run the joint venture. Management accountability could be assigned to one partner or to a team recruited from the companies involved.

- Avoiding undue interference from the partners

in the running of the joint venture: this is timewasting, and demoralizing to the management team.

It should be recognized at the outset that the objectives of the partners tend to change over the years. Eventually it may be desirable for one company to buy out the others, or to sell off the business, or even terminate it.

A Majority Stake

When acquiring overseas, there may be benefits in some countries to leave a minority stake with the vendors or even to invite a local partner to invest.

The local involvement in the business may be helpful in getting things done more quickly than a foreign company is able to do alone. Equally, customers may have a definite preference to buy from a company which is perceived to be 'local' to some degree.

When an individual shareholder is to continue as a director of the acquired company and retain a minority equity stake, it is preferable for the purchase contract to provide the option to buy out the remaining shares. Usually, the option would be for a period, and there may be a prescribed formula or mechanism for valuation to avoid disagreement later.

Performance-related Purchase

One way to purchase an unquoted company is to buy the entire equity for an agreed sum payable on legal completion. This may involve considerable risk to the buyer and, possibly, some disadvantage to the vendors where they are continuing to manage the business:

- The vendors would normally be expected to sign a contract and enter into a 'non-competition' clause. If the vendors have received a large payment for their equity stake, a service contract should not be regarded as a guarantee of their commitment to the continued success of the business.

  It is probably unrealistic to expect the vendors to work flat out for a business they have built up and sold, merely in return for a salary.

- If the business to be acquired has definite growth prospects, then the vendors may expect to share in some of the future success in return for selling the business now and providing continuing management.

One way to overcome the problem is a 'performance-related purchase' which is sometimes described as an 'earn-out'. This means that the vendors receive an initial sum and additional payment(s) dependent usually on pre-tax profit performance. Further payments are calculated according to a defined formula, normally over a period of one to three years, and occasionally up to five years.

Performance-related purchases are particularly relevant for the acquisition of service companies. In many cases, the assets to be acquired are only worth a small proportion of the purchase consideration. The real assets of the business are key fee or revenue earners who may leave, with the consequent loss of major clients and a substantial reduction in profits. In the circumstances, it is entirely reasonable that a significant part of the purchase consideration should be deferred, and the amount payable be dependent on future results.

Acquirers must recognize, however, that a per-formance-related purchase assumes that the business will be retained as a separate entity throughout the period of the agreement. If at some later stage during the agreement the acquirer wishes to merge the business with other activities, then this will require negotiation to terminate the performance-related deal prematurely, which may prove difficult and expensive.

Performance-related purchases offer infinite scope to devise and negotiate a deal. Experienced professional advice is necessary to avoid the pitfalls which may result. The simplest type of deal could be where the purchase price is dependent upon a given pre-tax profit being achieved for the current financial year. The vendors may agree to a sizeable sum being retained until the audited results are available. In the event that the required pre-tax profit is not achieved then the agreed deduction from the purchase price may be either a sum equal to the profit shortfall or based on a multiple. In practice, performance-related purchases may be much more complex. Careful design is essential to avoid undue incentive to increase profits by deferring necessary expenditure or by seeking undesirable marginal business.

Vendors should only be expected to agree to a performance-related purchase price if one of them has a service contract to continue as managing director of the company throughout the period in which payments are to be calculated. Otherwise the vendors are likely to regard the performance-related payments to be outside of their control.

Many vendors are understandably reluctant to agree to a performance-related deal. Sometimes, however, a performance-related deal may be the only way in which the vendors are able to obtain what they feel the business is worth. For example, a company formed in recent years may have penetrated an attractive market segment but only with the help of disproportionately high research and development or marketing costs. Profits may be small, or possibly losses may still exist, and the company may have to be sold because of the problems of arranging additional finance.

Whenever a performance-related purchase is involved, the contract document inevitably becomes significantly longer to protect both parties. For example, the vendors will wish to ensure that profits are not depressed by excessive management charges or unacceptable transfer prices when trading with other companies in the group. Conversely, the acquirers need to ensure that management services provided to the company are charged for at an acceptable rate. Additionally, to minimize the risk of misunderstanding later, it may be useful to discuss future operating methods with the vendors in some detail and to write a letter setting out any significant points which are not appropriate for inclusion in the purchase contract. An example could be a commitment to open a US sales office next year, and for which adjustments have been incorporated into the profit thresholds for calculating the deferred consideration.

Specialist tax advice should be taken to ensure that no unexpected taxation liability will arise from the performance-related deal being proposed, and that legitimate opportunities have been taken to minimize the tax burden on the vendors.

These are the options which should be examined before deciding on acquisition as the appropriate course of action. The following chapters deal with acquisition, either with or without a performance-related deal.

Key Point Summary

- Think hard before making a minority equity investment in an unquoted company. Negotiate an option to acquire majority or outright control at the outset, wherever appropriate.

- Consider a joint venture or consortium rather than rejecting an opportunity.

● Explore a performance-related purchase to reduce the risk of paying excessively for an acquisition.

4 Defining an Acquisition Profile

A research project showed that an average of one person year of work is spent for each completed acquisition, up to the time when the contract is signed. At first sight this may seem a surprising figure, but the author has found it confirmed by a number of companies.

Some prospective acquisitions will be aborted after considerable effort, and occasionally not until the final negotiation stage or even as a result of an unsatisfactory accountancy investigation. Also, completing an acquisition usually involves several people from the acquiring company, and there is the expense of using outside advisers.

The aim must be to minimize abortive effort from the outset. It is essential that divisional and subsidiary management are not allowed to pursue a specific acquisition candidate without board approval in principle. An approved Acquisition Profile is a key factor to help avoid unnecessary effort.

An Acquisition Profile is simply a written description of the important features required in a company to be acquired. It is a valuable aid to clear thinking, and should be signed by the appropriate director to authorize work to proceed. Two sides of paper are adequate to give a description which will focus the search for suitable companies. This means that companies which clearly fall outside the Acquisition Profile will be rejected with a minimum of time and effort.

The Acquisition Profile should describe both quantitative and qualitative features which are important to the acquiring company, even if some of them are subjective. For example, it may be considered essential for the existing managing director to continue running the business following the acquisition.

The content of an Acquisition Profile should include a brief description of the acquisition target in terms of:

- Market segments, products, services

- Commercial rationale

- Maximum cash available for acquisition

- Maximum total purchase consideration

- Minimum size

- Minimum profitability

- Management and management style

- Location

- Key requirements for success

● Financial returns to be achieved

Each of these items is described below to provide a basis for writing an Acquisition Profile.

Market Segments, Products and Services

A vague description, such as 'leisure' or 'electronics', is almost certain to result in wasted effort when searching for companies for acquisition. More importantly, it probably reflects a lack of clear thinking within the acquiring company.

'Leisure' embraces countless possibilities. After much wasted effort and delay, one company was helped to redefine the business description previously expressed simply as 'leisure'. The result was clear-cut and led to a successful acquisition. The new description was 'a chain of do-it-yourself retail stores, primarily with large out-of-town sites and ample car parking facilities'. The aim was to use the acquisition as the base from which to build a nationwide chain of do-it-yourself superstores.

Commercial Rationale

Many companies do not define the commercial rationale with sufficient clarity to focus the acquisition search. In the above example, a broader description such as 'do-it-yourself outlets' could have resulted in the acquisition of a chain of small high street retail shops, when the growth was forecast to occur in edge-of-town superstores.

Maximum Cash Available for Acquisition

This should take into account any cash requirements of the existing business and the likely needs of the acquisition over the next two years, which tend to be underestimated.

Maximum Total Purchase Consideration

If shares and/or some form of loan stock are to be offered for part payment of an acquisition, it is important to decide the maximum amount of 'paper' which should be issued.

In a group where financing is usually handled at head office, it is essential that a division or subsidiary should obtain approval of the maximum purchase consideration to be made available at the outset. The amount of funds to be provided to one subsidiary for acquisition is a matter for main board decision. The subsidiary cannot assume that the funds it generates will automatically be available for acquisition or that provided a target rate of return is achievable then unlimited funds exist.

Minimum Size

Many unquoted companies are overly dependent on one person, or at most two or three key people. This may represent a high degree of vulnerablility to the acquirer, at least until experienced management support can be arranged which often takes considerable time when diversification is involved. It is preferable that the size of the company to be acquired is sufficient for there to be some senior and middle managers currently employed in addition to the vendor shareholders.

It is generally preferable to make one sizeable acquisition, rather than two or more smaller ones, in order to achieve a given market share. The time spent in investing and negotiating more than one acquisition is considerably increased. Then there are all the problems involved in integrating and rationalizing two or more companies. Surplus directors and managers have to be removed or accept that they are to report to someone else. Operating procedures are almost certain to be different, and some uniformity of systems is usually necessary. One company supplying the retail trade expected this problem to be easily solved, only to find that to establish a common order-processing system involved a considerable outlay on computing capacity.

Minimum Profitability

A loss-making company with a given turnover is cheaper to purchase than a profitable one of similar size. It may be possible to buy a loss-maker at a discount on the book value of net assets, and yet it could prove to be a most expensive purchase.

Loss-making companies and businesses bought from a receiver need the immediate injection of a full-time chief executive. If such a person is not available, the advice must be not to proceed unless it is a start-up situation where losses are to be expected at this stage. Equally, it is not enough simply to appoint a chief executive on a part-time basis or to make someone available shortly. The person to be appointed should be involved in the investigation of the business, committed to the recommendation to acquire the company, and take up a full-time appointment immediately legal completion takes place.

Ideally, the chief executive appointed will have had experience of having turned loss-making companies back to acceptable levels of profitability. For maximum effectiveness, a suitably experienced full-time financial controller is needed from the outset to support the chief executive.

Otherwise, at least a tolerable level of profitability should already exist in the prospective acquisition; and the acquiring company should have definite ideas of what action is needed to achieve a satisfactory level of performance.

Management and Management Style

Compatibility of management styles is crucial for effective post-acquisition control success.

The criterion for deciding which directors and key executives to retain must be their ability to do the job in a way acceptable to the acquiring company. For example, some people manage unquoted companies successfully with a turnover of several million pounds by keeping key figures in their head or at most in a pocket notebook. Budgeting and monthly accounts may not exist. If the acquiring company regards these as essential disciplines, then discussions with the people concerned should take place before any negotiations commence.

Many people managing unquoted companies successfully find it difficult to change their management style and disciplines substantially. The acquiring company should keep change to an essential minimum and recognize that some flexibility can be a valuable aid to success.

Location

The location of a potential acquisition often needs to be considered from a practical point of view. It is better to think in terms of travelling time rather than distance. A journey time of up to two hours is fairly convenient. It means that people can visit the company and do a full day's work without the cost and disruption of staying away overnight.

Key Requirements for Success

There is no such thing as the perfect company, and least of all a perfect acquisition candidate. So it is a recipe for failure to seek the perfect acquisition.

Two or three key factors should be identified which are considered essential for success. These should be complementary to, rather than similar to, the strengths and weaknesses of the acquiring company.

For example, a retailer with an enviable reputation for in-store merchandising rejected an acquisition candidate primarily because the merchandising was poor. They failed to recognize that whilst merchandising was important to acquisition success, they had the expertise to provide the improvement needed.

In contrast, consider an electronics company wanting to broaden the product range by acquisition.

If the research and development skills involved are

different from the existing business then a strong development department may well be a key factor for success.

Financial Return to be Achieved

It is desirable to specify the financial return to be achieved. This might be expressed in various ways such as a maximum price earnings multiple, a required discounted cash flow rate of return or the minimum return on capital invested. The question of valuation is covered in Chapter 8.

Key Point Summary

- Write an Acquisition Profile to minimize abortive work.
- Define the products and services of the acquisition in some detail.
- Identify the two or three key requirements for success.

5 Overseas Acquisitions

Acquiring a company overseas needs particularly careful thought and analysis at the outset. It could prove to be an expensive ego trip. An overseas acquisition should be demonstrably relevant to defined corporate objectives and strategy.

There are strategic reasons, economic and political, for avoiding undue dependence on the economy of one country. It would be hoped that a depression in the home market would be partially offset by growth in overseas markets. For a company with a major share of the domestic market, overseas growth may provide the only substantial opportunity to develop the business. Politically, a business which is multinational is less vulnerable to threats such as nationalization.

There are serious risks involved as well: customer

resistance to overseas-owned companies; language difficulties; cultural differences and simply ignorance of local regulations can prove hazardous. An important foundation for successful overseas acquisitions is to stick to businesses in which the company has proven experience elsewhere.

It is important that alternatives to acquisition outlined previously are examined constructively, before the decision is made to pursue an acquisition.

Selecting the Country

Before an Acquisition Profile is written, the country for acquisition must be chosen. This involves much more than market considerations. Some of the key factors are:

- Political stability
- Cultural and social background
- Economic environment
- Legal requirements
- Taxation and repatriation of funds.

These are considered individually below.

Political stability

The importance of political stability depends upon the pay-back period for an overseas investment. If simply setting up an assembly facility in rented premises, then the pay-back period may be as little as two years. For an acquisition, the time scale is likely to be much longer.

The likelihood of political instability, civil unrest,

national strikes and local wars must be considered. A number of countries will be ruled out on this factor alone.

Cultural and Social Background

It is important that the country accepts overseas ownership of businesses, and the implications of capitalism involved. Evidence of this may appear by the extent to which foreign investors are treated differently from home investors. Some countries offer valuable incentives, whilst others visibly discriminate against foreign ownership. Standards of education and labour relations need to be adequate to support the type of business and the management style required.

Communications and services need to be adequate to support the business. Without these, achievement may be seriously hampered.

The safety of expatriate executives and the family lifestyle may need careful consideration. In some countries kidnapping is a hazard, and there is an unacceptable threat of violence both on the streets and in the home. Substantial insurance and precautions for personal safety may be essential.

Business practices and ethics vary enormously from one country to another. It may not be possible, for example, to operate effectively without paying bribes, ranging from the petty to the substantial, simply to get things approved or done.

Economic Environment

The ideal country will combine the prospect of attractive growth in the relevant market sectors, acceptable levels of inflation and a relatively stable currency. In some countries the general prospect for economic growth may be poor, while certain market segments still offer an attractive investment opportunity.

Legal requirements

Restrictions on the proportion of equity ownership by foreigners are widespread. In some countries equity control must remain with local shareholders. The key issue is management control rather than equity control. It may be possible to have effective management control whilst only having a minority equity stake. In such circumstances, it could still provide an attractive investment opportunity. Effective management control may require the expertise of expatriate executives, and in some countries there is strong pressure to replace them by nationals.

Official approval by government agencies will be required in most countries to complete an acquisition. Monopoly and anti-trust style legislation may exist. Local advisers are needed to steer a course to meet the legal requirements of the country.

Following acquisition, there will be local requirements to meet and these should be known at the outset. In addition to anti-trust rules, there may be exchange control regulations, employment law, reporting requirements and such like.

Taxation and Repatriation of Funds

The investment in an overseas acquisition needs to be evaluated net of taxes. Corporate taxation rates and incentives, tariffs, withholding taxes and double taxation agreements must be taken into account.

It is not necessarily enough to achieve an acceptable rate of return on the funds invested, net of taxation. The rules for repatriation of profits and capital should offer adequate scope for the movement of funds.

By considering the above factors, a satisfactory choice of country should be possible. Equally, it is necessary to check that enough suitable potential acquisition companies exist and that purchase price expectations are likely to be acceptable.

Companies for Potential Acquisition

Since the owner of an unquoted company is able to veto an acquisition approach, it is desirable to start out with a number of possible companies so that there is an acceptable likelihood of completing an acquisition. If the type of company to be acquired is likely to be quoted, then there should be at least two or three prospective candidates. If only one suitable company exists, regardless of whether it is quoted or not, it may be necessary to offer an unacceptably high premium over the current share price to obtain the support of their board.

Purchase Price Expectations

If sufficient potentially suitable companies exist, an early check of purchase price expectations must be made to avoid abortive effort. A comparison of price earnings multiples for the relevant industry sectors in the overseas country and the home stock market will provide a guide. This is appropriate for unquoted companies as well because relevant price earnings multiples tend to set a bench mark. By comparing price earnings multiples and recent completed acquisitions in the same sector, it should be possible to establish whether or not likely purchase prices will provide the bidder with an acceptable return on investment.

Key Point Summary

- Select the country for overseas acquisition first.

- Consider political stability; cultural and social background; the economic prospects; legal requirements; taxation and the repatriation of funds.

- Check there are sufficient prospective companies to acquire at an early stage.

- Find out the relevant earnings multiples in the country and market sector of interest.

6 Finding Acquisition Candidates

It cannot be stressed too much that any attempt to make an acquisition involves a substantial amount of time and effort on the part of directors and senior executives. There is a real danger that the existing business will suffer from a lack of attention.

There can be no guarantee that the reward for this effort will be a completed acquisition. Indeed, it would be unrealistic not to expect that some attempted acquisitions will be aborted for good reason when the work has almost been completed. This applies to the acquisition of both unquoted and public companies.

It must be recognized that some unquoted companies are unequivocally committed to preserving their independence and will reject any bid or merger approach whatsoever. But such a policy can change unexpectedly with, for example, the death of a key director or sizeable shareholder.

The search for potential acquisitions should not be restricted to companies which are known to be available for sale. Opportunism is essential, but an Acquisition Profile should prevent the purchase of a company simply because it is advertised or offered for sale; or it is thought likely to be receptive to a bid approach; or it seems to be a financial bargain.

The key factor is that the acquisition must be consistent with the corporate goals and direction as defined in the Acquisition Profile which is written before the search for potentially suitable companies begins.

The step from Acquisition Profile to a 'shopping list' of acquisition candidates may be a difficult one. If the acquisition is to be made in an existing market segment and geographic territory it is possible that all of the companies which fit the profile are known to the bidder. However, if a degree of diversification is involved the bidder will almost certainly not be aware of the companies which could be attractive. Some successful unquoted companies deliberately shun publicity in order to avoid being pestered by potential bidders.

A systematic search is recommended to attempt to ensure that every company likely to fit the Acquisition Profile is identified and listed.

Acquisition Search in the UK

The data on unquoted companies is well documented. Important sources of information are:

- *The top 4,000 Private Companies in the UK*

- The Extel cards for unlisted companies

- Financial surveys published on particular business sectors

- Regional surveys of unquoted companies

- Membership lists of the relevant trade associations.

On-line electronic database services are now available to provide unquoted company information. The search and classification capability of these services offers a labour-saving way to carry out a systematic search.

The database may enable a search to be carried out against a combination of criteria such as:

- standard industrial classification number for a particular business sector

- range of turnover

- minimum pre-tax profits

- minimum shareholders funds

One company used Yellow Pages with considerable success to identify small companies in clearly defined geographic areas as part of completing a nationwide network for their company.

Advertisements and editorial features on new products in the appropriate trade journals will reveal possible candidates. Trade exhibitions and special press features may also be a useful source for identifying companies active in the marketplace.

Some acquisitive companies complement the desk research outlined above with positive action designed to flush out companies which might be inclined to consider selling. For example, the chairman's statement in the annual report and accounts may make a brief but quite specific reference outlining acquisition intentions. Alternatively, the press release announcing annual or half-yearly results may refer to acquisition goals, even to the point of highlighting the search in the headline. Much will depend on whether or not the prospective acquirer could be harmed by competitors knowing of their intentions earlier than necessary.

Press advertising to find companies to acquire can be unproductive. Few people are likely to reply to a box number advertisement. It is essential to give the name of company, a person to contact and to invite telephone replies.

The objective is to identify the possible candidates as exhaustively as possible, and not to restrict the search to those thought likely to be available for acquisition. Published financial information may not be available for some of the candidates, such as divisions rather than subsidiaries of groups of companies. Figures for limited liability and public limited companies can be obtained by a search at Companies House, or by using search agents, although it should be recognized that the latest accounts filed may be up to two years old.

Staff such as buyers, senior sales people and technical experts should be briefed to report on any information or speculation which may pinpoint a possible acquisition target.

Once a list of possible companies has emerged, supported by outline information about each of them, further information may be obtained by continuing to watch the relevant trade and local press. Enquiries should be made concerning the products or services supplied.

A check should be made in *Who Owns Whom* to find out if any candidate is a subsidiary of another company. This would not necessarily rule out the company. Groups of companies often approach the sale of a particular subsidiary in an unemotional way, and it could well be that the business in question no longer fits their mainstream activity.

The search process must not be regarded merely as an important clerical job; far from it. The search needs to be carried out by someone with marked commercial perception. The outcome could be to identify a company which does not neatly fit the Acquisition Profile but is. even more attractive. If this happens, the Acquisition Profile should be reviewed. Equally, in some market sectors one may find no candidates which fit the Profile. This suggests that the Profile has been defined too tightly, or that no initial check was made to establish that enough potential candidates exist. The Profile must be reviewed and modified to reflect the actual situation.

The end result of the search is a 'shopping list' of acquisition candidates, perhaps categorized into a preferred short-list and a reserve list. At this stage, no approach should have been made to any candidates.

Acquisition Search Overseas

In acquiring companies overseas, the approach is similar to that described above, but the problem of distance has to be overcome. If the potential acquirer has an operation or regional office in the country concerned, this provides an effective base from which to mount a search. If not, the problem is to sustain the search process. In a large country such as the United States, there is a case for having an executive working full-time to co-ordinate the search in order to achieve success in a reasonable period of time.

Using Outside Help

A systematic search to identify acquisition candidates requires a concentrated effort for a short period of time, usually between about two to four months. Except for the larger and more acquisitive companies, it is probably unrealistic to create an appointment or department for the search task. The problem is to make a suitable person available without regular work suffering.

Outside help and contacts may prove helpful and cost-effective. There are several sources of help, including:

- Merchant banks and stockbrokers
- Business brokers
- Major accounting firms
- Specialist advisers

Merchant Banks and Stockbrokers

Only a few of these are prepared to undertake a systematic search for potential acquisitions on behalf of a client. Many do maintain a register, however, of buyers and sellers. A use of registers alone is not enough to ensure acquisition success, but equally it should not be ignored. The cost involved is likely to be a finder's fee, payable only if an acquisition results from an introduction.

Business Brokers

These range in size from established companies with a network of regional offices and overseas associates to individuals operating from home. Consequently there is a wide range of effectiveness to be found.

The best of the business brokers provide a valuable service. Some maintain extensive lists of companies either for sale or prepared to consider an approach. One or two are prepared to research a market segment to identify suitable companies and then approach them. Most brokers work on a 'no deal–no fee basis', calculated as a percentage of the value of consideration paid. So this can provide a way to complement in-house efforts to find suitable acquisition candidates.

Major Accounting Firms

Most of the major firms in the UK are part of a computerized database network designed to match relevant buyers and sellers. Additionally, it could be useful to notify receivership departments of an Acquisition Profile to ensure that as many people as possible know of the acquisitions being sought.

Specialist Advisers

Some specialist advisory companies, such as Livingstone Fisher Associates, offer advice and temporary executive help at various stages of the acquisition process. This could include helping the company to define the Acquisition Profile, to research a market segment, to identify acquisition candidates, and to approach short-listed candidates on behalf of the client. The work should be undertaken for an agreed fee, and any request for a monthly or quarterly retainer should be firmly rejected.

One benefit to the client is that the day-to-day management of the existing business does not suffer by diverting executive effort into acquisition search. Also, the specialist advisers may have a valuable network of relevant contacts not only within the industry sector but also amongst other professional advisors and financial institutions.

Key Point Summary

- Make a systematic search for target companies when a degree of diversification is involved.

- Use someone with commercial perception to carry out an acquisition search.

- Brief your buyers, senior salespeople and technical experts to report back on information which might pinpoint a potential acquisition.

- Notify banks, stockbrokers, accounting firms, specialist advisers and business brokers of the Acquisition Profile as part of the search.

7 Investigating a Potential Acquisition

Some background research should be done on each company on the acquisition 'shopping list'. The aim is to list or categorize the companies in order of preference before contacting any of them. Some companies will be eliminated on the basis of the information obtained. It is surprising how much information can be assembled without obviously contacting any of the companies. A little thought will generate several legitimate avenues for collecting background material, and some examples are given below.

In addition to obtaining annual accounts filed at Companies House in the UK, it is routine to obtain literature describing the products or services supplied.

Depending on the cost involved, samples of products may be purchased. If the products are sold through retailers or wholesalers, it is worthwhile visiting several outlets to see how display and promotion are handled at the point of sale. Copies of press advertisements should be collected. Trade press magazines may provide useful background information about the companies.

Once companies on the shopping list have been placed in some order of preference, the next step is to start contacting them. The initial approach to the company requires careful thought. If the acquisition candidate is in the same market sector, personal contact may already exist between board members from each company. In this case, informal contact may be possible in an atmosphere of mutual respect. Alternatively, a common acquaintance might offer an acceptable means of introduction.

The more difficult situation is when there is no personal contact between two companies, and this is often the case. Possible means of contact are:

By Telephone

Most potential acquirers would not outline their acquisition intentions during an initial telephone call. The purpose of the telephone call should be to achieve an informal meeting, perhaps over lunch. To avoid rejection at the outset, the reasons for meeting should be given in broad terms. For example, it could be described as a chance to discuss potential common interests.

By Letter

A carefully written and personal letter suggesting an exploratory meeting indicating an interest to acquire is received quite regularly by many companies. Some business brokers mailshot prospective vendors to locate companies for sale. The result is that many of these letters are put straight into the waste paper bin.

If the letter does not receive a reply, a follow-up telephone call is essential. Acquiring companies is a selling job, not a purchasing task, and one cannot afford to have any approach rejected without a determined effort. It has to be said, however, that a telephone call is more likely to produce an initial meeting than a letter.

By Third Party

A third party could be a specialist advisory body or a merchant bank. There should be a definite reason for using a third party. If the reason is to conceal the identity of the prospective bidder then it is important that the third party knows why. The potential vendors may have reason not to welcome the bidder's approach, and the third party will have to put forward a convincing argument at the initial meeting.

Prospective vendors may have a negative response to an approach by an overseas company, or have the impression that the acquirer will be prepared to pay an extravagant price for the company. A third party can help 'sell' the acquiring company to the vendors, and at the same time underline that any offer will not be unrealistically high.

One reason for using a third party is simply to save executive time. The company may wish the initial approach and an exploratory meeting to be carried out by a third party, so that their executives only become involved when it is established that a company on the shopping list is prepared to consider acquisition.

The chances of achieving an exploratory meeting are usually increased either by naming the client at the outset or by saying that the identity will be revealed at the initial meeting.

For many companies seeking acquisitions, there is a

scarcity of relevant businesses to acquire. So it is essential that a premature rejection by any acquisition target is avoided wherever possible. Some acquirers recognize that certain specialist advisers have developed a particular ability to cajole prospective vendors to agree to an exploratory meeting, and use such a third party simply to enhance their chances of success.

When either a listed group or an unquoted company receives an approach, even if totally unexpected, it should be considered seriously and constructively before making any response. There is nothing to be lost by agreeing to an exploratory meeting. In some cases acquisition has been rejected emphatically but some mutual and profitable business opportunity has resulted. Before this meeting, however, the vendors will have collected background information about the potential bidder and should have had a brief discussion with their professional advisers.

Whom to Contact

When wishing to acquire the subsidiary of a group, it is strongly recommended that the approach is made at group level. If contact is made with the subsidiary initially, it may simply put the idea of a management buy-out into their minds.

The person to contact in a large group is not necessarily the chief executive. His secretary is likely to suggest whom to contact.

When approaching an unquoted company, the managing director may be the wrong person to contact. It is essential to contact the controlling or largest shareholder. If there is an institutional shareholder, he may be able to offer advice on whom you should contact within the company.

Exploratory Meetings

Where the exploratory visit is made by a third party, this may provide an opportunity to outline key aspects of what the prospective bidder has in mind. For example, the bidder may regard it to be essential that the key directors are happy to continue running the business and to sign service contracts. Alternatively, if the bidder regards a performance-related deal to be essential then the idea should be introduced to the potential vendors as soon as possible.

The first meetings between the principals are of crucial importance. Unless and until a mutual rapport, trust and respect are beginning to be established, any other progress is largely illusory. There may be an immediate recognition by the prospective vendors of a worthwhile opportunity with tangible benefits for both parties. More likely, however, this stage of coming together will take several weeks or possibly several months.

The prospective vendors may state that they are not prepared to consider a sale for, say, another two years so that they are able to realize anticipated success. This could be a suitable occasion to suggest a performance-related purchase as a way to avoid delay by rewarding the vendors for future success. Whatever happens, the essential result of the initial meetings is that both sides should feel that they would be happy to resume a dialogue at some time in the future. The vendors may wish to consider other potential bidders, but may not actually say so. If the bidder appears to be too eager then his progress is likely to be one step forward and two steps back.

The purpose of the exploratory stage is to agree in principle that both companies wish to pursue the possibility of acquisition seriously. To avoid abortive effort, tentative agreement needs to be reached on several issues.

Broad price expectations need to be compatible, although it is difficult for the bidder to make a definite offer until the investigation of the company has been completed. The type of deal, particularly if it is to be performance related, and the preferred type of purchase consideration, need to be discussed. The intentions of key directors with significant share stakes need to be known before service contracts are offered. Any significant changes in management style and control should be explained and discussed.

When this degree of agreement in principle has been reached, the next step is to discuss the extent of information to be exchanged before detailed negotiations commence. The scope and nature of the investigation will need discussion and agreement. Prospective vendors are understandably concerned at the prospect of two or three people spending time in their premises to obtain confidential information.

The prospective bidder may reasonably ask for an assurance that the vendors will not be involved with other potential purchasers until the detailed negotiations have been concluded. The vendors normally require assurance of confidentiality and may ask the investigating team to pose as customers, auditors, bankers or insurance assessors.

The result of the initial approach may be a firm rejection by the reluctant vendors. In these circumstances, however, it is essential that the prospective acquirer terminates the meeting on a positive and friendly note. It should be agreed that the acquiring company will keep in touch from time to time, as the attitude towards selling the company may change rapidly as a result of, say, serious ill-health or the death of a key director and shareholder. Better still, every effort should be made to find a viable mutual business opportunity or even modest collaboration. At least this should provide a return on the abortive acquisition effort and even pave the way to acquire the company later.

On-site Investigation

There are two crucial points for the bidder to bear in mind:

- Desk research alone is quite inadequate
- Let the buyer beware.

A comprehensive investigation is essential before negotiating the purchase of a company. The purpose and scope of the task must be clearly understood. The objective is not simply to 'audit' or verify past performance, or even the current year to date. The aim must be to assess both the short- and medium-term future prospects as well. The art is that of prospecting for, and assessing, the gold ore still in the ground, not just counting gold bars in the vaults.

The essence of a successful acquisition investigation is to identify the vital factors for success in the business concerned, and to examine these in some depth.

On the negative side, one should be looking out for vulnerable features of the business and assessing whether or not the performance has reached a plateau or is about to decline. On the positive side, equal importance should be given to identifying latent opportunities for profitable development and any undervalued assets. For example, consider a stationery manufacturer selling mainly to individual retailers and wholesalers. There may be scope to appoint national accounts salespeople to sell to major chains of supermarkets and speciality shops. In unquoted companies there is a tendency to value stocks conservatively and this may represent a significant hidden asset.

Another important factor to assess during the investigation is whether or not the management styles of the companies are compatible. For instance, a requirement to operate complex and rigorous financial planning and control procedures may be unrealistic to people used to working in an informal way without any budgetary control.

Information obtained should not be restricted to financial data. The scope of the investigation must be wide enough to give an overall picture of the business, covering marketing, sales, research and development, manufacturing, administration, personnel and industrial relations.

The information should be sufficient to make future profit and cash flow projections as a basis for deciding the value of the company to the purchaser. Also, an assessment of the present balance sheet worth of the company needs to be made.

The investigation should only be regarded as complete when one can comfortably make a firm recommendation either not to proceed further, or to enter negotiations to complete the purchase. In the latter case, it is essential that the recommendation to proceed is supported by a list of key actions essential for the successful post-acquisition management of the company; for example, to appoint a marketing director because there is considerable scope for business development.

The Investigating Team

The selection of the investigating team is important. Possibilities include:

- Use an in-house team of about three people

- Use an in-house team complemented by an outside specialist

● Sub-contract the investigation completely, perhaps to a specialist team from a firm of auditors or consultants.

There are strong reasons against sub-contracting. The investigation is an invaluable opportunity for the people who will be responsible for managing or integrating the acquisition to gain first-hand knowledge of the business. Also, an outside team may be reluctant to report on uncertain and intangible aspects of the business, although these are often more important than features which can be measured accurately.

An in-house team should reflect a breadth of experience. For example, in a manufacturing business the team could be a marketing/sales person, an accountant and a production/technical person. It is important that the team members have had substantial operating experience at some stage in their careers. One person must be accountable for presenting a written report and a clear-cut recommendation either to proceed with negotiations or to terminate the matter.

The addition of an outside acquisition specialist to the team merits serious consideration. Such a person is particularly important if the in-house team members have little or no acquisition investigation experience. The outside person can be used to obtain particularly sensitive information, while the team leader maintains his personal relationship with the vendors.

One sensitive area may be the nature and extent of benefits enjoyed by the directors, such as the use of an expensive company-owned boat. The directors involved may object to being questioned on such matters by senior executives from the acquiring company. Another sensitive area may be relationships with trade unions. Persistent questioning, to the point of becoming irritating, may be needed to obtain an adequate picture.

Conducting the Investigation

The investigating team should either prepare or be given a checklist before commencing work on site. A basic acquisition investigation checklist is given in the Appendix. To this should be added any key features relevant to the particular business to be investigated: for example, the different official approvals awarded to an electronics company, without which it may be excluded from important sources of business.

Before the team visit the company, it is important that the chairman or chief executive has convinced the vendors of the importance and the scope of the investigation. The approach should be that the maximum offer can only be made if comprehensive information is available. The point should be made that it is only human nature to bid conservatively if relevant information is not provided and has to be guessed at. Nonetheless, the vendors are sometimes surprised by the scope and depth of information requested by the team. Quite often they are unable to provide the information and need time to collate material from the relevant records.

So it is recommended that the first visit by the investigating team is used to describe the information required in some detail. Undoubtedly some of it will not be available and an alternative approach will have to be discussed. The investigating team may offer to collate or analyse information from the prime records of the company if it is judged to be sufficiently important. Some selling, cajoling and negotiating may be needed to obtain agreement to provide sensitive information.

Occasionally the vendors will refuse to provide some essential information outlined during the first visit. If this happens, it may require a further meeting involving the chief executive of the acquiring company to resolve the matter amicably. Until the vendors have agreed to the scope and depth of the investigation required, it may be undesirable to commence any detailed investigation work on site.

The outcome of the first visit by the team should be agreement on the timing and conduct of the investigation. Following the investigation, which may take from one day to a week depending upon the complexity, a final visit should be arranged for about a week afterwards. This will provide an opportunity to clarify some points and ask further questions needed to complete the investigation report.

During the first visit, it is desirable to ask for copies of documents such as internal management accounts to be studied off-site.

The investigation stage needs sensitive handling. It is easy for the directors to feel they are being cross-examined and to be embarrassed by not being able to answer some questions. There are times when it is appropriate to back off a particular subject and return to it later.

One should not rely on opinions when the facts are available. Tactfully, but firmly, it is necessary to ask the directors to support their opinions with accurate, up-to-date documents.

Listed below are a few examples of problems which emerged during on-site investigations:

- An electroplating company — although there was scope for considerably increased business, the factory had almost reached the effluent limit set by the local authority and negotiations to increase the limit had failed.

- A capital equipment manufacturer — with a fourteen-month forward order book, at fixed prices, and including a totally inadequate allowance for the impact of inflation.

- An electronics company — dependent on a licence agreement to use a competitor's patented process for the major product range; a renewal of the licence needed to be negotiated within eighteen months.

- A trade distributor — without any written agreement with the major supplier to the business covering the exclusive distribution rights for the UK.

- An international service company — with two key appointments held by younger members of the family who were unsuited to the task and would have to be moved.

- A software company with nearly thirty managers and salesmen, having negotiated an endless variety of individual incentive schemes, mostly without an upper limit.

Clearly, most of the above examples would influence the amount one would be prepared to pay for the business in question, or in some circumstances would rule out the acquisition altogether.

Detailed note-taking by each team member is essential. Relying on memory is unacceptable. Each evening the team members should review the information obtained and plan the next day. Gaps in knowledge, inconsistencies in the information provided and requirements for further data must be identified.

Written projections for more than the current year are uncommon in unquoted companies. It may be appropriate to ask the directors to construct a profit forecast for the next financial year and to give broad sales projections for the following two or three years. The information and assumptions used as the basis for these forecasts must be known. Then the team should prepare their own profit and cash flow forecasts off-site reflecting their own assumptions and the impact of any changes to be introduced under new ownership. The investigation report should be completed as far as possible before the final visit is made to clear up any remaining queries.

The presentation of the report to the directors of the acquiring company needs thought. One method recommended is to circulate the report and then for the team to give an overhead slide presentation to the board. This should be followed by rigorous questioning of the team by board members.

If the decision is to proceed with negotiations to purchase the business, the next step is to formulate an offer based on a valuation of the business.

When the purchase negotiations have been completed, it is recommended that a firm of accountants are appointed to carry out an investigation of the company to be acquired. This should be completed prior to legal completion of the purchase. If anything seriously amiss is discovered, it is better to renegotiate the terms of purchase prior to completion rather than to seek recourse afterwards under the indemnities and warranties contained in the contract. If it has to be accepted that an investigation by accountants may only be carried out immediately following legal completion, then it is desirable to retain some of the purchase consideration until the work is completed.

Some companies simply ask a firm of accountants to carry out an investigation. This is unsatisfactory. It is like asking a builder to build a house without agreeing a specification. If the management have done their own on-site investigation, it will probably be an unnecessary expense, delay and disruption to the vendors for the accountants to assess the future business prospects of the company to be acquired.

The partner to be in charge of the investigation should be briefed at a meeting, and the scope of the study confirmed in writing. The aspect to concentrate on should be defined, and also those to be regarded as outside of the scope of the investigation. After the investigation report has been received and studied, a debriefing meeting should take place with the partner concerned to clarify any queries and to gain further insight.

Key Point Summary

- Carry out background research on target companies before contacting them.

- Plan carefully how to contact each company to avoid a premature rejection of the approach.

- Check broad price expectations are compatible before doing an on-site investigation.

- Include in the investigation team those who will either be managing the acquired company afterwards or supervising the investment.

- Provide the investigation team with a detailed checklist for their work.

8 The Valuation and Offer

It is premature to decide how much the company is worth or what to offer until the question of what to buy has been answered. The following case of a light engineering company illustrates the point.

The company sought help to investigate, evaluate and negotiate the purchase of a loss-making subsidiary of a quoted company. The intention was to purchase the share capital, and agreement in principle had been reached with the prospective vendors.

The specialist advisers probed the commercial rationale of the proposed purchase with the client. The subsidiary was made up of three quite separate businesses, although these were not designated as divisions. One business was making a modest profit and was of strategic importance to the client. The second operation was breaking even, and it made more sense for the vendors to keep this as it was a major user of raw material supplied by another subsidiary. The third business was making heavy losses and there appeared little likelihood of breaking even without drastic surgery. Closing down the operation appeared to be appropriate as a reasonable return on investment seemed improbable over the medium term.

The advisers convinced the client that purchasing the whole subsidiary was not appropriate and would be unnecessarily costly and time consuming in post-acquisition management. Several meetings with the vendors took place. Finally the vendors agreed to keep the second business as a user of their own raw material and to close down the loss-making operation. This was in their own interest when it became clear that the client was only prepared to purchase the relevant business and would pay an attractive price.

The outcome was dramatically more acceptable for the client. The plant, stock and trade marks of the relevant business were purchased, instead of the equity of the subsidiary company. Only a quarter of the total floorspace was required and a medium-term lease was negotiated. To purchase the freehold land and buildings would have cost more than two million pounds. The relevant employees were offered jobs and the business is succeeding.

Whilst the vendors had the problems and cost of closure, this eliminated a long-standing situation which would have become worse. When the deal was announced, the reaction of the stock market brought about an improvement in their share price. There is no doubt that the purchase of the whole subsidiary could have been negotiated and completed more quickly than the deal which was actually made. But the executive time saved and the return on capital achieved fully justified the delay.

When dealing with a receiver, the question of what to purchase should be considered carefully. Obviously, the receiver would prefer to sell the whole business as a complete package. If there are several businesses making up a group, the receiver may be prepared to sell them separately. It is important to explore this. Even if the company in receivership is one business, there may still be room for manoeuvre. In a recent example, the purchaser persuaded the receiver that one product line was of no interest because the product was almost obsolete. The receiver agreed finally to exclude the equipment and stocks from the purchase of the business, and to sell these items separately at whatever price could be obtained.

The aim in any acquisition ought to be to buy the income generating capacity of the business, with the minimum of unwanted assets or peripheral activities. Often it will be necessary to buy the whole business, but wherever appropriate the issue of excluding unwanted assets and activities should be explored.

Valuing the Company

The essential point to recognize is that there is no single, correct answer to the question of how much a company is worth. The buyer and seller are initially likely to have significantly different views.

Basis of Valuation

The starting point for a purchaser to calculate the value of a target company should be to:

- assess the present balance sheet work and the realistic value of any surplus assets;
- project future profits and cash flows.

Future projections of profits and cash flows need to be based on rigorous analysis. It is recommended that the most recent audited profit and loss account of the target company is related to reflect:

● the accounting policies of the acquirer — e.g., the treatment of items such as depreciation and the valuation of work in progress may be different.

● different operating standards and cost levels of the acquired company — e.g., the needs for greater insurance cover; higher wage and salary levels; additional pension contributions.

● realistic rewards for the directors — e.g., lower salaries which may be agreed to by continuing directors to bring them into line with group policies; the savings resulting from the termination of relatives employed in the business and no longer required; eliminating the cost of unnecessary extravagances such as aeroplanes, boats and overseas homes used by directors.

The next step is to make realistic projections of profits and cash flows for the target company in current and future years, on the basis outlined immediately above. The benefits of synergy arising from the acquisition should be calculated and shown separately. Otherwise, there is a risk that these benefits will be included to justify too high a valuation.

The aim should be to purchase the target company at a valuation which retains most of the benefits of the synergy to be obtained for the acquirer.

There is a widespread tendency by acquiring companies to exaggerate the amount of synergy to be gained and the speed with which it will occur. Estimates of synergy should only be made after identifying:

● what specific action is to be taken,

- who will do it,
- how quickly it will be done,
- what extra costs of implementation will be involved,
- what tangible financial benefits will result,
- how quickly these will commence.

Criteria for Valuation

The yardsticks most widely used to value an unquoted company include:

- the earnings multiple
- discounted cash flow analysis
- return on capital employed
- impact on earnings per share
- asset backing

It is recommended that at least two of the above methods are used to arrive at a valuation of the maximum price to be paid for a target company.

Use of Earnings Multiples

The price earnings ratio, or earnings multiple, of a company quoted on the stock exchange is the number of years of profit after tax per share which the current market share price represents. For example, if the share price is 150p and the profits after tax per share last year was 10p, then the earnings multiple or price earnings ratio is 15.0.

If the target company is large enough to justify entry to the stock market, the price earnings ratio that the shares would command should be assessed by a comparison with other quoted companies in the same industry sector.

As there is significant cost and time required to obtain a stock market quotation, the likely price earnings ratio of the target company should be reduced by about 20 per cent to reflect the fact there is not a market in the shares at present.

If the target company is not large enough to be quoted on a stock market, the likely price earnings ratio should be reduced by between 20 and 50 per cent. The amount of the reduction should reflect the attractiveness of the particular business sector and the scarcity of suitable target companies available to purchase.

Some large quoted companies, experiencing a relatively low price–earnings ratio for their shares, would like to think that they will not need to pay a higher price–earnings ratio valuation to buy a relatively unknown unquoted company than that of their own shares. This can be quite unrealistic. If the target company is in an attractive business sector into which the acquirer wants to diversify, offers the prospect of rapid profit growth, and there is a scarcity of suitable companies to acquire, it is likely to command a higher price–earnings ratio valuation than the quoted bidder.

Price–earnings ratios for stock market companies are shown each day in the leading financial newspapers, calculated on the reported profits after tax for the most recent financial year. Sometimes the advisers to vendors of unquoted companies will seek to apply a price–earnings ratio to a forecast of current year profits in order to justify a higher valuation for their client. Unless the financial year of the target company is virtually over, valuations based on current year profit forecast should be firmly rejected by acquirers.

Discounted Cash Flow Analysis

Some companies carry out a separate valuation using

discounted cash flow analysis to ensure that cash is given sufficient emphasis.

DCF is a relevant concept for acquisition evaluation. The purchase consideration for the acquisition is equivalent to the capital expenditure for a project. The net annual cash flow for each year can be calculated by aggregating the cash from operations with the working capital and capital expenditure requirements.

The residual value of the assets should be taken into account at the end of the period of evaluation, in the same way as this is done when using DCF to evaluate capital expenditure projects within a business.

In this way, the acquisition can be evaluated by calculating the percentage internal rate of return which will be achieved for a given purchase price, and comparing this return with the appropriate yardstick used by the company.

Whilst DCF is conceptually attractive and relevant for evaluating a proposed acquisition, the risk of significant error in forecasting cash flows for several years into the future must be recognized. Consequently, it is unwise to rely exclusively on DCF as the basis for acquisition valuation.

One of the important benefits of DCF is, however, the facility to calculate answers to 'what if' questions easily. For example, there may be a risk to an advertising agency that it will lose a client as a result of a conflict of interest arising from the proposed acquisition. The 'what if' facility allows the rate of return to be quickly recalculated on the assumption that the client would be lost.

In some situations, such as acquiring a loss-making company which can be turned around into profit quickly, the calculation of discounted pay-back period may be appropriate. Expressed simply, this means calculating the number of years required to generate sufficient cash to recover the purchase price, after taking into account the cost of interest on the cash required to finance the acquisition.

Return on Investment

Many groups of companies use the pre-tax return on capital employed as a key measure of performance for each of their subsidiary companies. So it is not surprising that some chief executives use a similar approach as a short-cut method to assess a prospective acquisition.

The pre-tax profit forecast for the target company, as assessed by the acquirer, is divided by the expected purchase price. The answer gives a percentage pre-tax return on the proposed purchase price. It must be realized, however, that this simplistic approach does not take into account the financing cost of the purchase consideration to be used to buy the target company.

If the expected purchase price does not produce a satisfactory return in the current year, then the question to be answered is how long will be required to achieve the required return based on projected profit and cash flow forecasts. Hard-headed chief executives are likely to demand that the required rate of return should be achievable in the next financial year, and certainly no later than the second year following acquisition.

Impact on Earnings per Share

The rate of growth in earnings per share year by year is a key determinant of the share price of a quoted company. So if the acquisition is likely to have a significant impact on earnings per share because

- the target company is sizeable in comparison to the acquiring group,
- the proposed purchase price values the target

company at a significantly different earnings multiple than that of the acquirer,

- the cost of overdraft or loanstock interest to finance the purchase will depress net earnings

then the resultant earnings per share figures should be calculated taking into account the overall impact of the acquisition. This should include the effect of subsequent deferred payments to be made as part of an earn-out deal and the impact of the conversion of any convertible loanstock issued as purchase consideration.

Asset Backing

The asset backing of the target company, taking into account the estimated market values for land and buildings, should be calculated as a percentage of the purchase price. For a service company such as an insurance broker, estate agency, sales promotion consultancy or computer software house, the asset backing as percentage of the purchase price may well be less than 25 per cent.

If the bidder has a strong asset backing and is looking for earnings growth, then an acquisition providing considerably lower asset backing may not be especially important, provided that the overall dilution of asset backing is not excessive. It must be realized, however, that the future success of a service company employing, say, 150 people may be unduly dependent on the continued commitment of a mere handful of the present owner-managers. In these circumstances, performance-related purchase or an earn-out deal offers some protection to the purchaser.

When buying a loss-making company or a business in receivership, the aim should be to acquire it at a discount to the value of net assets to be acquired at the time of purchase. If the business is making losses at the time of negotiation, the further diminution in net asset value by the time of legal completion must be assessed and reflected in the offer. The further discount to be negotiated must adequately reflect the continuing losses which are inevitable after the purchase until the business can be turned around into profit.

Other Valuation Factors

The value of a company to a prospective purchaser should not be reduced simply to the calculation of financial yardsticks. The cash flow and profit projections need to be carried out rigorously, the financial yardsticks calculated, and then judgement must be applied.

It may make sound commercial sense to pay more than financial criteria alone would suggest because of:

- strategic fit,
- rarity value or uniqueness,
- defensive need.

An example of strategic fit would be where a chain of retail outlets was weak in a high-growth region of the country, and one particular target company existed which would meet the need. Rarity value, which in the extreme case could amount to uniqueness, could be in an attractive niche market such as the provision of specialist computer training courses where the market leader is an unquoted company.

A defensive need could be where a natural product market leader is faced with the threat of a patented, biotechnologically produced low-cost alternative from an unquoted company. In these circumstances, the purchase price needed to acquire the company should be evaluated in terms of the aggregate impact. This means assessing the purchase price on the basis of the *sum* of the incremental profits and cash flow which will result if the acquisition is made *and* the decrease which will occur if the target company remains independent.

Worth to the Vendors

Some vendors argue, understandably, that the worth of their company is simply the highest sum, net of tax, obtainable from any potential bidder. An investigation of 'comparable' acquisitions reported recently in the financial press may provide some ammunition to support a higher valuation for the business.

There is no correct valuation. Negotiating experience, judgement, 'nose' and horse-trading skills all have an important impact on the final outcome. Nonetheless, the vendors should use the valuation techniques described in this chapter to calculate a realistic expectation of the worth of their business.

Formulating The Offer

From the valuation calculations, the amount of the offer should be determined. The aim should be to arrive at an opening bid figure and the maximum amount which could be paid. It is vital to fix the upper limit before negotiations commence and the figure should be authorized in writing as a discipline.

If this is not done, too high a price may be paid simply to avoid losing the deal. An actual example illustrates the point. The bidder had improved the opening offer substantially to £5.1 million. The vendors offered to sell at £5.2 million. The bidder was not prepared to lose a deal of this size for £100,000 and accepted. However, if a maximum figure had been set before negotiations began and emotion took over that figure would have been nearer to £4 million.

Key Point Summary

- Negotiate exactly what is to be purchased, before attempting to calculate a valuation.

- Assess the balance sheet worth of the target company, and forecast future profit and cash flows as the basis for valuation.

- Use a variety of methods to calculate the maximum value of the target company; such as earnings multiples, discounted cash flow analysis, pay-back period, return on investment and asset backing.

9 Negotiating the Purchase

During the exploratory meetings between the chief executives there should have been some discussion of the likely price range and preferred form of payment, in order to establish at the outset that it should be possible to reach an agreement in due course. The wishes of the vendors concerning their future role in the business also needs to be explored at this early stage.

If the acquirers were determined to negotiate an earn-out deal from the outset, this should have been agreed in principle during the exploratory meetings. There are occasions, however, when it is only as a result of doubts and uncertainties arising from the investigation of the target company by the management of the acquirer that the need to pursue an earn-out deal occurs. Equally, the management investigation of the target company may cause the tentative, initial valuation to be changed significantly. Other issues which could materialize are the need to terminate some people's employment, the need to close a branch or depot, or the requirement that one of the shareholding directors should cease to work in the business after the acquisition.

Following the completion of the management investigation of the target company, there is a strong case to have a preliminary negotiation meeting to talk about the broad shape of a possible deal in terms of:

● factors arising from the management investigation which alter the valuation;

● the revised thinking about likely purchase price, if appropriate;

● the period of any earn-out deal and the proportion of purchase consideration to be paid initially;

● confirmation of the form of purchase consideration;

● continuing directors, those retiring, and any consultancy agreements;

● the need for any redundancies amongst the staff;

● the purchase of any assets of the company by the directors — for example, boats and second cars;

● any other issues the vendors wish to raise — for example, delaying legal completion for a month so that it takes place during the next fiscal year and will delay the payment of capital gains tax by a year.

At the end of this preliminary negotiation meeting, it is important to agree a date and a venue for the final negotiations to take place. It should be established that, on the agreed date, either a deal will be agreed in detail and solicitors instructed, or the negotiations will be terminated. This means that the vendors should arrive at the final negotiation meeting fully prepared and with their professional advisers present. There needs to be the overt agreement to agree a deal on the day or to walk away.

If the vendors' professional advisers are consulted after the final negotiation meeting, which was allowed to take place in their absence, the response is almost certainly likely to be that negotiations should be re-opened in order to obtain a better deal for the vendors. This situation must not be allowed to happen.

Preparation for Final Negotiations

The location of the final negotiations is important. Any interruption or distraction, such as a telephone call, should be avoided. It may therefore be preferable to use a nearby hotel or professional advisers' premises rather that the vendors' offices. A separate room is required to which either party can retire from the negotiations for a private discussion.

Final negotiations often take several hours, so an early start should be made to allow a full day for discussion if necessary. A sandwich lunch delivered to the negotiating room is desirable. This avoids losing momentum in the negotiations and saves time.

The acquiring team need to prepare an agenda for the final negotiations. The aim should be to cover all of the issues necessary to produce a comprehensive agreement with the vendors. It is totally unsatisfactory to simply agree the purchase price and the outline of an earn-out deal, only to leave the solicitors to resolve the other items.

A typical agenda for a final negotiation meeting is:

- Update of events since the previous meeting.
- Retirement package for one of the directors.
- Service contracts and any consultancy agreements for continuing directors.
- The basis of an earn-out deal.
- Service contracts to be negotiated with key employees.
- Company assets to be purchased by the shareholders.
- Leases of premises used in the business but owned by the vendors as individuals.
- Visit to a key customer before legal completion.
- Any particular conditions, warranties and indemnities.
- Purchase price.
- The timetable to legal completion.

An effective ice-breaker to start the final negotiation meeting is to ask the vendors to give an update of significant events since the previous meeting. Valuable information may be gained as well: for example, confirmation that the results shown by the latest management accounts are as expected, that the level of order intake is being maintained, or that a major new customer has been obtained.

When the acquirer requires that a director should

retire early on legal completion, the retirement package needs careful negotiation. It must be established that any compensation for loss of office is a part of the total purchase consideration. It is important that the negotiation of retirement package is placed early on the agenda so that each of the shareholders agrees a realistic figure knowing that this will directly affect the purchase price.

Every effort should be made to agree salary levels, compatible with group salary policies, for shareholders who are to continue working in the business. If the vendors have previously enjoyed excessively high salaries, which reflected their ownership of the business, then the profit impact of their accepting realistic salaries should be reflected in the valuation of the business. The length of service contracts needs careful thought. In most circumstances, a one-year service contract, renewable by mutual agreement or terminated by either side at six months' notice, is sufficient. Acquiring companies have made expensive mistakes by giving three- or five-year contracts to shareholder directors. Within a year of making the acquisition, they want the vendors to leave and find themselves having to pay off the contractual commitment.

Certain key employees of the company may be poorly paid by job market standards and employed on the basis of only one month's notice to terminate their employment. The acquiring company may require that they have the opportunity to negotiate new contracts with them before legal completion of the acquisition.

Company assets to be purchased by the shareholders could include boats, aeroplanes and motor cars for relatives. If the vendors are to be allowed to purchase these at advantageous prices, then it should be pointed out that this benefit is part of the overall sum to be obtained from the sale of the business.

Sometimes premises used by the company are owned by the vendors as individuals. Quite often in these circumstances there is no formal lease, and the terms of one will have to be negotiated or a purchase price agreed, if appropriate.

In some businesses, one customer may represent a significant part of the total turnover. If this is so, it may be necessary to negotiate that the acquiring company will be allowed to meet the customer in the last few days before legal completion.

Key conditions, warranties and indemnities may need to be established at the final negotiating meeting, rather than left to the solicitors to agree between themselves. Examples would be the insistence to have a retention of some of the purchase price for a period to reinforce the warranties and indemnities, or that the net assets at completion date will be in excess of a given figure.

It is only at this stage of the negotiation that the purchase price should be discussed and agreed. A maximum figure should be set before the meeting, and if a deal cannot be done within this limit then the appropriate action must be to walk away rather than to horse-trade upwards.

When an earn-out deal is involved, the specific details to be agreed include:

- the period of the earn-out deal,
- the accounting policies to be used to calculate profits,
- management charges to be made by the group,
- cost of finance provided by group,
- costs of using central service departments — for example, group transport.
- pricing policies for intra-group trading,

- commercial features which will affect profits — for example, the need to appoint a qualified finance director and the commitment to open a US sales office.

- pre-tax profit targets,

- a formula to calculate the amount of deferred payments.

Before the meeting is concluded, if a deal has been agreed, then a timetable should be set to cover the events leading up to legal completion. The steps involved include:

- receipt of the draft purchase contract by the vendors and their advisers,

- commencement of the investigation by external accountants,

- completion of the investigation,

- preliminary meeting between the solicitors to both parties,

- a date reserved for both parties and their solicitors to meet, in order to resolve any outstanding points in the purchase contract,

- receipt of the disclosure statement by the acquiring company,

- date and venue for legal completion.

Both parties must realize that the verbal agreement is subject to contract and usually to a satisfactory accounting investigation as well. There is no place for celebration until legal completion takes place. Only then is it appropriate to drink champagne with the vendors.

Heads of agreement are misunderstood by some people, because these are only an agreement to agree, subject to contract and to satisfactory accountancy investigation, in the same way as the verbal agreement. The signing of heads of agreement is not binding; but psychologically the vendors may feel more committed to complete the deal.

On most occasions, however, a summary of the agreement, written in commercial terms, is a sufficient record of the agreement reached. It is not necessary to have heads of agreement drafted by solicitors.

Negotiating Skills

Some people are natural negotiators, others either intensely dislike negotiating or are mediocre at it. The negotiating team should be chosen on ability, not seniority within the acquiring company. Most people working for large companies have little opportunity to develop acquisition negotiation skills, whereas a professional adviser may be involved in negotiating deals every week.

Some general points of guidance are given below.

To Vendors

- Obtain expert advice on the most tax-effective form of purchase to suit your own circumstances. Particular attention must be paid to minimizing capital gains tax liabilities for sizeable shareholders.

- Recognize the legal complexities involved and ensure that you choose a solicitor experienced in this specialist kind of work.

- Do not be hurried. Take professional advice before negotiations commence, and, most importantly, have an adviser present, or available on call, during the negotiations.

- Spell out what aspects of the sale are important or desirable to you at the outset.

To Bidders

- Before discussing the features of a deal, spell out the mutual benefits; the proposed method of working together; any different reporting or authorization procedures; and any major changes to be introduced in the foreseeable future.

- Do not make an initial offer which is so low that the vendors are likely to terminate the negotiations prematurely.

- If the future success of the company is susceptible to changes such as the departure of a key director or a licensing agreement not being renewable, take this into account and seek whatever protection is available.

- Recognize that the success of post-acquisition management is often influenced by the manner and spirit in which negotiations are carried out.

- Avoid a competitive bid situation. Seek a verbal commitment from the vendors that they will negotiate only with your company unless they decide that the final offer is unacceptable.

- Before negotiating, decide on the maximum worth of the business to your company, and do not exceed that figure unless the prospects or circumstances change significantly.

- If no agreement is reached, ensure that both sides feel that they would be happy to resume negotiations if circumstances change. Absolutely nothing is gained by an acrimonious failure to agree.

Key Point Summary

- Agree the broad outline of the deal in a preliminary negotiation meeting and set a date for final negotiations.

- Have a comprehensive agenda to guide the final negotiation meeting to a successful completion.

- Agree the terms of employment for any vendor shareholders continuing to manage the business first.

- Negotiate any consultancy contracts, termination payments and purchase of company assets next.

- Agree any terms and conditions which may affect the valuation before negotiating the purchase price.

- Remember that the agreement to purchase usually becomes binding only on legal completion, and have a definite plan to complete the legal work as quickly as possible.

10 Post-Acquisition Management

Successful post-acquisition management commences with the investigation of the target business by the team from the acquiring company long before the purchase contract is signed.

The way in which this investigation is carried out reveals the management approach and competence of the acquiring company, for better or worse. During this stage, working relationships should be established with key personnel of the company to be acquired.

The negotiations are equally important to future relationships. It is important that the negotiations are conducted in an amicable way. There is no place for acrimony or ill feeling. Those directors who are to continue working for the company should feel that an equitable deal has been negotiated.

Announcing the Acquisition

While the legal work is being completed prior to signing the purchase contract, there is an opportunity to obtain advice from the vendors on the most effective way to announce the acquisition. If any directors are to remain, they should be actively involved in the announcement and help to reassure people about the change of ownership. It is important that all employees are notified promptly and do not have to find out from either the newspapers or their trade union representatives.

The first day under new ownership is unquestionably the most important. Not only should meetings take place with managers, but equal importance must be given to discussion with trade union and shopfloor representatives. If it is feasible, a mass meeting of all employees is an effective method for communication and reassurance, as rumours will abound.

It is unwise to make commitments to employees about future prospects. The new management may well be asked for an assurance that there will be neither redundancy nor relocation within the next twelve months. Such an assurance cannot be given responsibly in most circumstances, even if there is no intention to take this kind of action. The only assurance that can reasonably be given is that if it should become necessary, there will be as much notice as possible and full discussion with the people affected.

There is merit in rehearsing the questions which are likely to be asked and the answers to be given. It would be naive to think that every awkward question will be identified, but this does not detract from the usefulness of the exercise. Where an acquisition involves simultaneous meetings in different locations a preliminary briefing is essential to ensure that a consistent message is put across.

If there is likely to be some adverse trade union reaction towards the acquisition, it may be useful to circulate a note summarizing the key points arising from initial staff meetings to avoid misunderstandings later.

Customers, suppliers and business associates should be notified promptly. Whilst initial notification will probably need to be done by letter, this should be followed up by a personal visit or telephone call to key people. To avoid delay, the preparatory work involved should be carried out between verbal agreement and the signing of the contract.

Managing the Acquisition

Effective communication with the board and senior management of the acquired company is the first step. It is important that they understand

- The commercial strategy to be pursued by the company acquired

- The approach to managing and developing the business

- Limits of authority and reporting relationships

- Personnel policies and philosophy.

Effective authorization of expenditure is essential from the outset. Purchasing limits must be set, and approval given before the order is placed. It is too late simply to authorize invoices for payment; the expenditure has already happened. Approval should be required for all recruitment, including the replacement of people leaving, to ensure that maximum use is made of available resources.

Effective control of pricing is equally vital. Any proposed amendments to published price lists, fee rates, or discount structures require the appropriate authorization. Similarly, quotations to be made at non-standard margins require prior approval.

A key appointment is the chief financial officer of the acquired company. A competent person is not enough. It is essential that the person acts in the interests of the new owners and does not allow past loyalties to affect his judgement. If there is any doubt on this score, then there may be a case for transferring the person to another appointment within the group, regardless of his competence. The situation must be dealt with according to need, not sentiment.

Senior managers must be given the opportunity to raise and discuss problems which they feel need to be tackled. They should be encouraged to put forward their ideas for developing the business and improving their performance. Good ideas may have been rejected by the previous owners without adequate justification or explanation.

Post-acquisition management requires much more than simply attending meetings. It is important that the acquiring company has a definite plan at the outset, with individual accountability clearly understood. No time should be lost before the key functions of the business are examined by the appropriate managers from the acquiring company. A programme of exchange visits can be used to achieve the understanding required in an acceptable way.

Financial Planning and Control

The accountants of the acquiring company need to think carefully about their priorities. It is tempting to press for standardized reporting procedures to be adopted quickly. Effective cash management, together with prompt and reliable monthly profit figures, should be the first priority. Then attention should be focused on short-term sales and profit forecasts. Standardized formats for presentation can come later.

Unless financial planning and control are well established, it is more realistic to defer the introduction of new reporting formats until the next financial year commences. The accountants of the acquiring company need to demonstrate their patience and to recognize that an important part of their contribution is likely to be in an educational role.

Key Point Summary

- Involve any continuing directors in the announcement of the acquisition.

- Hold discussion meetings with directors, management and staff on the first day of ownership.

- Have a definite plan to learn about the business; attending board meetings is not enough.

- Concentrate initially on the essentials of financial control, namely: cash management, monthly reporting and short-term forecasting.

11 How to Turn Round Loss-Making Companies

A successful executive may be appointed at short notice to take charge of a once profitable company which is now operating at a loss. His job is to achieve a turnround to profit. The approach needed to turn a business round is significantly different from managing a profitable company. As speed is essential in any turnround operation, this executive must have a proven framework for tackling the problem.

When he takes up his appointment, his first impression will probably be that everyone appears to be busily occupied. It is unlikely that losses have been caused by lack of effort on the part of either workforce or management. The problem is more likely to be one of directing effort, rather than of increasing it; in other words, ensuring that people throughout the business are geared to achieve results and do not mistake movement for action.

The first and urgent task is to ensure the company is not trading illegally and that sufficient finance is available in the short term to enable the company to survive.

The existing management will probably expect and want immediate action from the new person. Furthermore, they expect the action to be tough. The turnround executive will be rightly concerned about his ignorance of the company which he has just joined. Radical organizational change or the switching of key personnel, if implemented too quickly, might prove to be inadequate or misguided measures in the months to come. Nonetheless, some impact can be made immediately, for example:

Temporary Help

Terminate all temporary help immediately, and fill the resulting gaps by redeploying existing permanent staff. If this causes a real problem, someone will scream loud enough. In the end the business is unlikely to suffer.

Indirect Staff

Insist that the recruitment of all indirect personnel (which are part of the company overhead), including replacement staff, will need chief executive approval before any action is taken. Review all indirect staff recruitment in progress. Stop all hiring except where an exhaustive check of existing staff reveals an unquestionable need.

Direct Labour Recruitment

If there is any likelihood that some redundancies will be necessary in due course, even the recruitment of direct labour should require chief executive approval.

This applies particularly in those countries where production labour costs should realistically be regarded as a fixed cost in the short term, and not as a variable one, because of the difficulty and cost of terminating any employee.

Fixed Assets

Insist that all capital expenditure above a given level is approved by the turnround executive. Wherever possible, delay non-profit projects such as the replacement of staff dining room equipment, refurbishing car parks, etc. Ask that unused plant and machinery be identified with a view to disposal, and that under-utilized floor space be measured so that the use of facilities can be rationalized in due course.

Inventory

Ensure that significant purchases against anticipated special orders receive chief executive approval. Material and piece part purchases should be allowed to proceed normally when covered by firm orders or when part of a standard product specification. Ask that all redundant stocks be identified and vigorous attempts made to dispose of the surplus at whatever price can be obtained.

Offices and Office Equipment

Cut back sharply on the redecoration of offices and the replacement of office equipment such as typewriters. The order of the day should be to make do and mend wherever financially justified.

Personal Cars

Delay, wherever possible, the replacement of cars supplied and maintained by the company, and keep the authorization of additional cars to an absolute minimum.

Foreign Travel

All foreign travel should require chief executive approval. In one actual example, the marketing manager had arranged a three-week visit to Brazil in order to assist the local distributor to expand sales. A request for a visit programme listing the companies and executives to be visited quickly established that no such planning had been done. The approval was deferred until such time as the local distributor had been requested to arrange an effective itinerary and been allowed time to carry out the preparation. Six months later the application still had not been resubmitted.

Entertaining

Check expense claims to ensure that any entertaining of clients is not unnecessarily lavish. There is more at stake here than the cost of the entertaining; in a loss-making company many employees just feel bitter when they hear about expense of this kind.

The impact of a series of immediate actions such as those above, which in no way makes an exhaustive list, really gets the message across that the decks are being cleared for action. The objective is to make the most effective use of the human and material resources already employed in the business. Admittedly, the impact of these actions is likely to more important in terms of the effect on employee attitudes than on profitability and cash flow; but some tangible improvement will almost certainly have resulted. Clearly, the turnround executive will want to reduce the list of actions requiring his approval as soon as he feels confident that his values and standards are shared by his management team.

Now the turnround programme may be started in earnest. The first task is to understand what is happening in the business, before taking precipitate executive action. What is more, the answers necessary for short-term success are likely to be found amongst the middle and senior managers of the company. The key questions to be asked of people by the turnround executive are as follows:

- What key factors are stopping you and the business being more effective and successful?

- What inexpensive and simple action would have a substantial effect on the performance of the company?

- What extra help do you need to do your job more effectively?

- What tasks could be eliminated altogether or made simpler and more effective?

- What is not being done that needs doing urgently?

Managers are often able to highlight a key problem area or opportunity in another department of the company while not being able to see scope for improvement in their own job. The turnround executive needs to be a good listener who neither takes sides nor apportions blame.

Start in the Sales Department

Even in a high technology company there is the strongest case for trying to understand the fundamental problems facing the business by examining the sales activity first. Almost by definition, a loss-making company cannot claim to be market-oriented. Ideally, every sales employee should regard his job as helping to provide outstanding service to present customers and anticipating the future needs of both established and potential customers. In working to achieve this state of affairs, there is no effective substitute for making field visits with salesmen, visiting agents and distributors, calling upon important customers, potential customers and even important established users of competitive products. Not enough can be learned about sales and marketing operations by attending board meetings.

Two weeks spent in the field represent an excellent investment of the turnround executive's time at this stage. In this way, first-hand information can be obtained about the product quality, service and delivery performance. Price competitiveness, the benefits offered by competitive products, the effectiveness of sales and distribution networks will begin to be understood as well.

Attention should next be focused on sales office and sales support services. The time already spent in the field will prove invaluable in asking the relevant questions about the effectiveness of sales support. A good starting point is to check how effectively action is taken on letters and telephone calls from customers. Operating standards are vital. Enquiries and orders should be acknowledged the same day. Complaints and requests for after sales service require particularly prompt attention. It is essential to notify the customer of the action being taken without delay. General correspondence, too, should be handled within two or, at most, three working days. When a telephone query cannot be dealt with on the spot, a promise should be made to call back by a given time, and that promise must be honoured.

Clearly, the effective handling of correspondence and telephone calls is not a panacea for the sales ills confronting a business. The attitude of mind that creates this type of effectiveness, however, is a prerequisite for what needs to be achieved in the coming weeks and months.

The turnround executive will then want to evaluate other important aspects of the sales operation. His previous management experience and his newly-gained knowledge of the present business will indicate which aspects require attention at this stage. They may include some of the examples given in the following list:

- The existence of adequate targets, incentives, operating standards, training and supervision for the sales force

- The liaison between the sales and manufacturing departments to ensure that the various customer demands and priorities are met in a cost-effective way

- The finished goods stocking policy used to ensure a balance between meeting customer orders from stock and the attendant cost of holding the inventory to achieve this goal

- The acceptance of orders for customer-made products as opposed to standard ones, and the basis for assessing the costs involved and the price to be charged.

- The responsibility and basis for offering one-off, cut-price or discount deals

- The extent to which the sales people participate in helping to collect overdue accounts from customers.

This is an intentionally simple approach, based on finding out exactly what happens rather than installing sophisticated management systems and controls.

Successful turnrounds are usually initiated by executive action ensuring that a few simple but important things are done outstandingly well. Installing some basic management controls should wait until this first stage in recovery has been effected.

It may appear somewhat illogical to investigate the sales activity before tackling the broader issues of the market-place and marketing; the reason for this is pragmatic. Even a sketchy knowledge of the sales effort, problems and opportunities will lend considerable perspective to one's understanding of the marketing challenge facing the business. Important marketing aspects to be looked at include:

● Any major products or services in the research and development stage for which there should be a clear-cut work programme through to product launch with an attendant expense budget

● Business development, including efforts to identify and pursue new products, territories, market segments, distribution and promotion opportunities.

● The effectiveness of sales promotion, advertising and exhibition expenditure

● The liaison between marketing and R & D to ensure that research projects are based on a market-oriented assessment of customer needs and provisional product specifications

● The extent, relevance and value of market research activity and data within the company as a basis for future business development

● The possible need for reduction in the range of products/models offered to the customers to ensure compatibility between market needs and the cost-effective use of production resources.

The Function of Finance

Time is of the essence, and it is therefore highly desirable that the groundwork in financial planning and control should be started at the same time as the turnround executive begins to look at the sales activity. Ideally he will have an experienced financial manager assigned to the business full-time for a given period. If this is not possible, then the turnround executive must be able to give instructions to the existing financial controller as to precisely what financial information is required.

From the outset, the role of the finance function is to provide other members of the management team with a service which is designed to make a tangible contribution to profitability and cash flow. In a turnround situation the real need is for sufficiently accurate figures produced promptly. Immaculately presented historical figures may be interesting, but represent a luxury at this stage. Forecast figures are invaluable as a basis for executive action.

There must be a dual attack on both profitability and cash management. While a budget may exist for the remainder of the current financial year, the turnround executive will be more interested in a month-by-month updated forecast of the detailed profit and loss account, compared with the original budget for the rest of the year. Ideally this will be presented to show both the percentage and amount of marginal profit contributed by each major product. Similarly, an updated cash flow forecast is needed weekly for the next month at least, then monthly for the remainder of the year.

Forecasts and Objectives

This forecast must be prepared on the basis of consultation between the line managers and the finance staff. It must be the line manager's own forecast as processed by the finance department, not an accountant's view alone of what the future holds. With the help of this simple financial picture, the turnround executive will be able to highlight the most significant areas of the business to be attacked first, whether these are sales revenue, marginal profit levels, product costs or overhead expenses. Obviously the turnround executive is seriously handicapped until these updated forecasts are available, and the senior finance staff should be expected to work flat out to produce them, with whatever overtime working is necessary.

The financial forecasts, plus consultation with line managers and finance staff, will no doubt show up a need for a series of *ad hoc* financial analysis exercises, to be completed quickly as the basis for short-term management action programmes to improve both profitability and cash management. Clear-cut deadlines for the completion of this work should be agreed with the finance staff.

By now the turnround executive will have been in charge of the business for thirty days or so. He will have been getting to know his management team, and they will have seen something of his management style, values and standards. Now is the time to set about translating the forecast for the remainder of the current year into firm objectives. Each member of the management team should be asked to present his revised objectives for the rest of the year, translated into financial figures with the help of the finance staff, and backed by a specific management action programme, together with a statement of any key assumptions incorporated.

These statements of revised objectives should be presented to the turnround executive for discussion, review and approval within a further fifteen days. This allows another fifteen days for revision and compilation of an overall business plan for the remainder of the current year. This means that sixty days after taking up his appointment, the turnround executive and his management team have an operating plan for the remainder of the year, backed by management action programmes and a statement of key assumptions. By this time too, the management team will realize that an operating plan is a commitment to achieve certain results, subject only to uncontrollable and unforeseen factors. It is an expectation and not merely a target or a forecast.

A Close Look at Administration

While the management team is preparing its objectives, the turnround executive spends his second thirty days having a detailed look at the remainder of the business, including administration, manufacturing and R & D. Administration takes priority because in a turnround situation it can represent a very real burden. In looking at administration expense, in the broadest sense, the turnround executive should have value analysis concepts very much in mind. He will be asking himself, and others, the reason for each administrative activity, using the type of questions which follows:

- Is the work necessary to meet statutory, legal or fiscal requirements?

- If not, what detriment would there be to the business in either the short or long term if the particular task or department was eliminated?

- If the work still appears necessary, who benefits internally, and is the existing service the most cost-effective and relevant approach?

- Are any administrative departments overstaffed or staffed to meet a peak demand?

- Is there any administrative work not being done which would represent both a tangible benefit and a net overall saving to the business?

At the end of his learning period the turnround executive should have got across the message that empire-building and status symbols are out. The order of the day is to provide a service which represents value for money.

The Manufacturing Angle

The turnround executive may never have worked in a manufacturing department, but this must not deter him from taking an earnest look at the activity. In the same way that he must go out into the field to appreciate quickly the sales and marketing problems, it is necessary to spend time on the shopfloor and in the warehouses to begin to understand the manufacturing challenge facing the business. Good housekeeping is important in a manufacturing operation. It is not just a question of tidiness. If management and workforce alike do not take a pride in their surroundings and adopt high standards, they are unlikely to take pride in the quality of the products supplied to customers.

On his very first visit to each location the turnround executive should not hesitate to point out any lack of good housekeeping and to expect rapid action to improve the situation. Once again the premise is that a major improvement throughout manufacturing will need a basic change of attitude at the outset. During his visits to the manufacturing departments the turnround executive will constantly be asking fundamental questions: Why? How? and What? The specific questions he needs to ask may include:

- What are the major constraints holding back

increased output and productivity, quicker and more reliable delivery performance, better product quality and reliability, and reduced inventory levels?

● How can we overcome these contraints in the most effective and inexpensive way in the shortest time possible?

● What should be done to improve the working conditions, motivation and morale of the workforce? How much will this cost? What other savings can be achieved to pay for it?

Research and Development

There is a strong temptation for the turnround executive to avoid getting to grips with the R & D activity because of his lack of technical expertise. The temptation must be resisted at all costs. He can perfectly well admit his ignorance of the technology involved, provided that he demonstrates a willingness to appreciate the problems and to take a lively interest in the work of the department. This approach will almost certainly enhance the respect he has already earned. Questions he will want to ask may include:

● Who initiated each R & D project currently in progress?

● What budget and programme exists for each project? How does actual performance compare with the original budget and programme?

● What financial return is expected from each project? What market research data is this based on? What product specification and price profile has been agreed with marketing and defined as the objective?

- What existing projects should be examined with a view to termination?

- What new projects should be initiated? For what reason?

- What is the allocation of R & D resources between basic research, new product R & D, and the improvement of existing products? Does this allocation meet the future market opportunities and competitive challenges facing the business?

- What is the current level of sales and marginal profit contribution derived from products emanating from in-house R & D?

- What R & D work is sub-contracted to other organizations? Which projects or specific tasks should be sub-contracted in future?

The Way Ahead

By now the turnround executive has spent sixty days getting to understand the business and its markets. He has initiated short-term action programmes by requiring firm objectives for the rest of the current financial year from his management colleagues. Now he must start to introduce more fundamental and long-term change. One important action is reviewing the organization structure and deciding what changes, if any, are needed. At the same time he should be ready either to confirm the selection of each member of his management team or to announce his alternative plans. The turnround executive will need a simple approach to organization. His aim will be to achieve a compact management team, with clear-cut accountabilities and the most direct lines of communication possible from top management to every employee.

Reducing the Workforce

At the same time, he will have decided in broad terms

the extent of staff reduction needed and will be ready to discuss his views with the management team. With luck, he will not have had to dismiss people during the first sixty days. A piecemeal approach to reducing the workforce has a devastating effect on morale. Nevertheless, if the situation was sufficiently serious to warrant earlier redundancies, then no doubt they would have been enforced.

Each member of the management team should be asked to produce a list of people either to be made redundant or transferred internally. The information required in addition to the names of the people affected is their job title, length of service, annual income, contract of employment and the cost of termination.

This part of handling a turnround situation is undoubtedly the most unpleasant aspect of the job. The executive reluctantly responsible for this task must do his utmost to ensure that people are treated fairly, and as generously and compassionately as possible. Failure to recognize the need for a reduction can only result in putting the jobs of everyone in the business at risk.

One thing the turnround executive must ensure is that the scheme to reduce the number of staff covers the entire business, from workforce through to senior management; otherwise a top heavy organization may well result. Clearly, however, to meet the future needs of the company some departments will suffer heavier cutbacks than others.

The next aspect to be stressed is confidentiality and security. If anyone other than the turnround executive's secretary does the typing and copying, the information might as well be put on the company noticeboard. Detailed planning should be carried out to arrange for all severances to be notified and executed at the same time, so that uncertainty and anxiety among the remaining personnel can be kept to a minimum. Equally important, appropriate notification should be given to trade unions and government departments in accordance with the highest standards of custom and practice of the particular country.

Budgeting

The preparation of a budget for the coming financial year offers an opportunity to pursue further the installation of effective short-term management within the business. The management team has by this time had the experience of making a commitment for the current financial year and fulfilling that commitment.

The finance staff have been directed about the scope, methods and format required for financial planning, control and forecasting in the coming year and will be ready to implement this, starting with the preparation of the annual budget. Each member of the management team will be expected to back his budget commitment with a quantified management action programme and a statement of the key milestones to be achieved on business development projects. This will ensure that there is a balance between the amount of executive time spent on day-to-day management problems and that invested in pursuing projects to achieve further profitable growth.

A Worthwhile Future for the Company

Despite the effective implementation of manpower reduction, improved operational management and the initiation of business development projects, the anticipated return from the funds invested may still be unacceptable in the medium term, even if operating losses have been eliminated. The turnround executive must not see the extent of his job as being the elimination of losses. That is only the first step, and often the easier one. The second stage is to achieve an acceptable return on the funds invested, or to dispose of the business as a going concern.

If the need for achieving a turnround has resulted from long-term changes in the marketplace in which the company operates then it will almost certainly be necessary to reposition the business. This involves a planned withdrawal from unprofitable products, services, market segments and territories and developing or acquiring alternative business which offers profitability and future growth. The repositioning of a business can take place in several ways. For example, the company could decide to look for future growth in, say, Europe; or it could concentrate on developing a higher quality, higher priced product range; or it could develop its ability to sell custom-made products profitably. A further option may be diversification to an extent which requires either a joint venture or an acquisition.

While the turnround executive may discuss his ideas on this subject with other managers, and may well invite their suggestions, the responsibility for decision rests squarely on his shoulders.

In the end, he may come to the conclusion that the business should be sold as a going concern to another company better placed to make an acceptable return from the funds invested. If so, he must have the courage to present the facts to his board for approval. It must not be seen as a statement of failure. In the final analysis, the management of opportunity is more rewarding than the management of problems, from the standpoint of shareholders, managers and employees alike. Once approval for disposal is given, then the turnround executive should expect to be actively involved, and probably personally accountable, for identifying prospective purchasers and successfully negotiating the sale of the business in conjunction with specialist advisers.

Throughout all this the turnround executive must learn to cope effectively with the uncertainty, anxiety and fear felt by workforce and management alike. He must be a person of integrity with outstanding management skills and, above all, the ability to communicate. It is important that he should appear cheerful, assured and poised at all times. If he appears to be despondent or out of his depth the effect on morale may be shattering. Both management and workforce will look to him for confidence and reassurance. His approach should be like that of the dentist who, at the outset, describes to the nervous patient the nature of the treatment he or she is about to receive and then explains each step as he goes along.

Two other aspects of communication are important—making promises and dealing with rumours. From the very start the turnround executive must not make any promises which are either beyond his control or beyond his present horizons. It is not unusual to be asked on the first day if an assurance can be given that there will be neither redundancy nor plant relocation within, say, the next six months. At this stage, the turnround executive is not able to give such an undertaking. The other feature of a turnround situation is the proliferation of rumours from top to bottom of the organization. Rumours must be flushed out into the open as quickly as possible, and a statement made by the management. Rumours left undealt with merely fuel the anxiety which already exists.

In conclusion, it can be said that every turnround situation presents a unique set of problems. There are no ready-made answers. The outcome of a successful turnround is defined as achieving an adequate return on the total funds invested in the business, and not simply as the elimination of losses. The methods, outlined for handling the situation successfully are based on taking effective executive action rather than concentrating on improved management control systems and procedures. The key to success is to concentrate on doing a few simple but important tasks outstandingly well, and to communicate confidence and reassurance to all employees, from shopfloor to boardroom.

Key Point Summary

- Make an initial impact by eliminating, reducing or deferring discretionary expense items, e.g. temporary help; personal cars and office equipment.

- Approve all recruitment because the aim must be to avoid hiring people at this stage.

- Start tackling the problems by spending time in the sales department, before assessing the market and examining marketing activity within the company.

- Produce a financial operating plan for the remainder of the current financial year within sixty days.

- Carry out all termination of staff employment on one day to minimize the impact on morale.

- Remember the goal is to achieve an acceptable return on the funds invested, and not simply to eliminate losses.

- Concentrate on doing a few simple but important tasks outstandingly well: this is the key to a successful turnround.

12 How to Make Successful Management Buy-Outs and Buy-Ins

Management *buy-outs* are commonplace in the USA and the UK, the largest examples running into billions of dollars. The American expression 'leveraged buy-out' is more accurate than the term 'management buy-out', because most of the finance is usually provided by institutions.

The members of the management team normally:

- invest some of their own money, often borrowed against the equity in their homes or with the collateral of insurance policies;

- obtain a significant equity stake in the company, disproportionately much higher than their personal investment of cash;

- can increase their equity stake by achieving

performance targets, often referred to as a 'ratchet mechanism';

- have executive management control of the business, although the financial institutions usually appoint one or more non-executive directors to represent their interests.

In the UK, management buy-outs have grown rapidly (the largest ones having cost several hundred million pounds each), and more than one hundred financial institutions provide finance for them.

In contrast, management *buy-ins* are less common in the UK, but are increasing. A management buy-in requires a proven track record in a closely related market sector. Some successful buy-in teams have consisted of only two people, usually a chief executive and a finance director. The first step is to find a suitable target company which can be purchased.

Management buy-outs and buy-ins offer attractive opportunities to managers because:

- Financial institutions want to realize their investments within five years, by selling the company or obtaining a stock market quotation. If an attractive opportunity to realize the investment arises much earlier, usually they will want to take it unless the management can convince them of the extra benefit from retaining the investment longer.

- The record of success has been very high, but of course there have been disappointments and failures.

- Managers have multiplied their original investment tens of times in the most successful cases.

Buy-outs and buy-ins really do offer the opportunity to create substantial personal capital within five years.

The initiative for a management buy-in must come from the managers themselves, and many buy-outs also arise from the initiative of the management team. Groups are prepared to consider divestment, including management buy-outs, for various reasons, including:

- the business is an unwanted part of a larger acquisition;

- it may no longer fit into the present commercial rationale for the group;

- the business may be too small to carry the overhead costs associated with a separate profit centre of a large group;

- the market is simply too competitive to carry the full weight of corporate overhead;

- the need to generate more cash or the wish to invest the proceeds in other opportunities.

Other opportunities for management buy-outs, and possibly buy-ins as well, include:

- privatization of state-owned corporations

- the purchase of a listed company, particularly where there are substantial family share-holdings and members of the family are approaching retirement

- an alternative to an unwelcome bid for a listed company

- purchase of a company in receivership.

Despite the availability of opportunities, and the substantial potential rewards, common sense demands that a hard-headed and objective approach is adopted by the management team.

Suitable Companies for Management Buy-out or Buy-in

The essential ingredients for a suitable company are:

- a positive cash flow
- adequate asset backing
- the business
- the management team

Each aspect will be considered in turn.

Cash Flow

Cash flow is the most vital consideration. Unless it is demonstrated that sufficient cash can be generated to pay the substantial amount of interest and repay loan finance when necessary, a deal is not possible.

It must be realized that the reason why the management team obtains a much higher proportion of equity than its members' contribution to the total funding is because a substantial amount of loan finance and overdraft facility is used to make the purchase. So a business which is likely to need significant injections of cash during the next few years is unsuitable for a buy-out deal. This means that businesses in relatively mature industrial sectors are usually more suitable than those in young, high-growth and high technology sectors, unless such a business can be managed in a way to generate cash: for example, by using distributors to stock the hardware and to install complex electronic systems which would require a substantial amount of working capital. However, in that case, the distributors are making a sizeable share of the profit the company could be making for itself, but profit is secondary to the need to generate sufficient cash flow to service the loan capital.

Asset Backing

As a substantial amount of loan finance and overdraft facility will be used to finance the purchase, it is essential that there are sufficient net tangible assets in the business to provide an acceptable level of security for the lenders. Service companies that are low on asset backing and heavily dependent on retaining key fee-earners may well be unsuitable. Not only is there the lack of security for the lender, but there is an added risk that key people, who are not part of the management team making the investment, may leave. Increasingly, whole teams of people leave companies either as a result of headhunting or to start their own business. In either of these circumstances a significant proportion of their clients may follow them.

The Business

A suitable company must have a long-term future. The sale of the business, or obtaining a stock market quotation, could take up to five years. Then the purchasers or new investors will want to see continuing prospects, so the cash flow generated has to be sufficient to pay interest charges, to provide for investment in replacement equipment and new technology in order to remain competitive, and to improve existing products and develop new ones where necessary.

The business may be making only a modest profit, producing a loss or be in receivership at present. This does not necessarily mean the company is unsuitable. A clearly thought-out plan will be needed, however, to show how sufficient profit can be achieved to help generate the necessary cash flow. Factors which may make this feasible include:

- eliminating central service charges and providing the necessary facilities within the business at a much lower cost,

- identifying specific and achievable cost-reduction opportunities,

- defining opportunities to generate additional turnover from the existing facilities.

Significant amounts of business with other group companies may be a cause of vulnerability. The management team should not expect favoured treatment as an independent company.

The Management Team

People talk glibly about management teams. Management teamwork is essential for a buy-out or buy-in. Members of the team need to be a close-knit group, totally committed to turning their vision of success into a reality.

Investors look for credibility in the management team. If the business is presently producing unsatisfactory results, the investors will want to know why and how the same people will be able to achieve a turnround. A competent financial director capable of ensuring cash-flow discipline is essential, but there should be no key appointment missing from the management team. If the technical director has just left, for instance, this may have caused a serious weakness that will not be easily overcome.

Making the Approach

Management buy-outs and buy-ins will be considered separately, as different approaches are required.

Management Buy-outs

The commitment of the chosen management team and their willingness and ability to raise some personal finance must be established conclusively at the outset. Otherwise, an unnecessary risk is being taken. The group may be upset at the suggestion of a management buy-out, and there is no point in taking the risk unless there is a determination to proceed.

One way to avoid this risk is for a specialist adviser to enquire whether or not a group is prepared to sell a business, without disclosing the identity of the bidder unless the group is prepared to consider a deal. This kind of approach is made frequently on behalf of corporate acquirers and is becoming increasingly common for management buy-outs. It is reasonable to expect the external adviser to make the initial approach without charge, unless agreement to proceed is obtained.

Management Buy-ins

A management buy-in requires a different approach, for the target company may be listed on a stock exchange. When an approach is made to a target company, whether or not it is quoted on a stock exchange, the prospective vendors will want an assurance that sufficient funds are available before exploring a possible sale of their business. It is important that the management buy-in team has made contact with prospective investors before contacting a target company. In this way they will be more convincing to a prospective vendor and able to complete the deal more quickly. Additionally, some buy-in investors know of companies which would be amenable to an approach, provided that a suitable management team is available.

Using an Outside Adviser

There is likely to be a strong tendency to reject outside advice and help in order to minimize expense, but the management team should recognize that it is facing a number of new challenges. They must be able:

- to negotiate the purchase with their present employers on equal terms, knowing that if a deal does not take place they will wish to remain as employees;

- to obtain the necessary corporate finance and taxation advice to decide upon the maximum price which should be paid for the business and how to structure the tax deal effectively;

- to select a suitable institutional investor from the large number available;

- to present themselves, and their business plan, convincingly to prospective investors;

- to negotiate the best deal for themselves with the institutional investor;

- to choose a firm of company commercial lawyers experienced in these deals.

An outsider adviser should play a leading part in tackling the above challenge successfully. The advantages which he should provide include:

- making an anonymous initial approach to the parent company,

- providing the valuation and corporation tax expertise needed,

- taking a tough negotiating stance with the parent company when necessary,

- choosing the three or four most relevant buy-out investors, from the dozens which exist, for the management team to meet and to make their personal choice of financial partner,

- having enough experience to know how attractive a deal can be negotiated with the investors on behalf of the management team,

- recommending a partner in a law firm with relevant experience.

The choice of institutional investor is important, for it involves much more than negotiating a one-off financial transaction. The investor will wish to appoint a non-executive director, possibly the person in charge of the investment or someone from its pool of available non-executive directors. It is important that the person appointed is compatible with the management team. Ideally, he should make a positive contribution to the business and not merely be a watchdog.

The choice of institutional investor will be put to the test if things start to go seriously wrong. The investor will want to see prompt and vigorous corrective action taken. In choosing among investors, therefore, the management team should ask how they have responded in situations where a company has faced a serious setback. The approach of different institutional investors varies widely: some are prepared to be patient, passive and tolerant, whereas others may seek to intervene decisively.

As an indication, three or four months should be sufficient to complete the transaction from initial agreement in principle. If the deal is in response to an unwelcome bid for a listed company, then a quicker completion is likely to be essential.

Business Plan

The purpose of the business plan should be to provide the information and forecasts for:

- institutional investors to help them decide to invest
- the purchase price to be decided
- the financial structure of the deal to be determined

The plan should be written by the management team, and must provide a comprehensive picture. The outside advisers should provide guidance and review it to ensure that it is an effective document to help sell the deal to investors.

Investors do not expect everything to go according to plan, so they expect to see:

- risk areas and uncertainties identified
- plans to avoid potential problems, or to minimize their impact
- contingency plans if problems do occur
- sensitivity analysis to answer 'what if' questions

The presentation of the document should be professional, attractive and readable; it should be bound effectively, and there should be an index. Published material such as product literature and press comment should be included in an appendix. The temptation to go into too much detail, resulting in too long a document, must be avoided. The first page of the plan should give a one-page executive summary of the entire proposal. All this may sound like common sense, but basic errors are often made. There may be no executive summary, the size of investment required may not even be mentioned, and duplicated copies of published material may be difficult to read.

The content of the plan should include:

Timescale

Once a buy-out or buy-in has been agreed in principle, speed is essential, or the business is likely to suffer. Uncertainty may lower morale amongst the staff. Less attention will be given to managing the business whilst the negotiations are taking place.

- An executive summary: a single page which tells the prospective investor in outline everything he needs to know to decide whether or not he is interested.

- The company:
  — history
  — present ownership
  — location
  — key products and services
  — suitability for a buy-out or buy-in
  — commercial rationale for making the proposed investment

- The marketplace, marketing and selling:
  — the size of the marketplace and forecast growth

—   competition and a comparative assessment of products and services in terms of performance and pricing

—   major customers and distributors

—   marketing, selling and sales promotion plans

● Manufacturing and distribution:

—   land and buildings

—   production facilities

—   use of technology

—   surplus capacity

—   need for additional capital investment

—   key suppliers and sub-contractors

—   warehousing and distribution

● Technical information:

—   current and proposed R & D projects

—   patents, licences and trade marks

—   anticipated technological developments within the industry and the planned response

● People:

—   members of the buy-out team

—   organizational structure

—   other key employees and expertise

—   headcount analysis by department

—   employee relations and trade unions

● Financial summary:

—   estimated purchase price and expenses

—   anticipated time to realize the investment and likely exit routes

— working capital requirements

— historical and forecast profit and loss accounts and cash-flow figures, covering the next three years

— budgeting, monthly reporting and financial management procedures

The appendices should include the following information:

● Detailed financial projections of profit and loss and cash flow for the next three years, supported by a statement of all assumptions used and sensitivity analysis.

● Management biographies: factual biographies of each member of the buy-out or buy-in team and other key managers and staff. Qualifications, previous employers, positions held and tangible achievements should be detailed. Waffle should be avoided.

● Published information:

— product and service brochures

— press comment and articles.

Negotiating the Deal

There is much more to be negotiated than simply agreeing a purchase price. The deferral of part of the purchase consideration, the structure of the deal, tax implications, conditions, warranties and indemnities may significantly affect the total cost and attractiveness of the deal.

Where the company is not listed on a stock exchange,

the first matter for negotiation is an exclusive option period. This means that an auction situation will be avoided. If there is a competitive bid, the purchase price required is likely to be higher. In addition, the added uncertainty may well damage morale within the company.

Key matters to be resolved, in addition to the purchase price, include:

- the use and cost of central services which will be needed for an interim period until alternative facilities are created within the company, e.g., data-processing;
- rights to intellectual property such as patents, trademarks, trade names and licences;
- the cost of any redundancies;
- the transfer of pension scheme benefits;
- the structure of the deal and the tax implications for both parties;
- warranties and indemnities.

In most cases, tough and expert negotiation is needed to achieve a satisfactory price for a buy-out or a buy-in. The burden of debt interest means that there is usually a fine dividing line between an acceptable purchase price and one which prohibits a deal altogether.

When agreement has been reached, the investors and lenders will normally require an accountants' report to be prepared by a suitable firm. It is the accountants' report, rather than the business plan, on which the investors will formally commit themselves to invest.

In the case of a buy-out, the management team's knowledge of the business, which it has used to prepare the business plan, should mean that there are no significant adverse disclosures in the accountants' report. In a management buy-in, however, the business plan has to be written much more on an arm's length basis, so there is a greater likelihood that the deal is renegotiated or the financial structure amended as a result of the accountants' report.

Staff

Motivation and morale should improve following a management buy-out or buy-in. There is a risk, however, that a 'them or us' attitude could develop, separating the management team that has invested in the business from the remainder of the management and staff.

Serious consideration should be given to creating staff incentive schemes on the completion of the deal. Depending upon current tax regulations, attractive incentive schemes may be provided by:

- profit-sharing
- share options
- saving-based share purchases

It is nothing less than enlightened self-interest to err on the generous side when creating incentives for management and staff in either a management buy-out or buy-in deal.

Key Point Summary

- Consider initiating a management buy-out of your company, provided that a positive cash flow can be generated and sufficient asset backing exists to support the necessary borrowing.

● Consider a management buy-in of a suitable company in an industry sector in which the team have proven experience.

● Recognize that cash-flow management is crucial in any buy-out or buy-in.

● Use external advice to help negotiate the best deal.

● Consider setting up profit-sharing and equity incentives for staff at the outset to ensure maximum co-operation and commitment.

Appendix: Checklist for an Investigation

Listed below is the basic information generally required in a pre-acquisition investigation. To this should be added any items which are relevant to the particular case.

Documents Of Which Copies Should be Obtained:

Memorandum & articles

Annual return

Audit report

Tax computations, agreement reached, notice of hearings

Directors' service contracts

Pension scheme

Bonus and share incentive schemes

Typical contracts of employment

Union agreements

Land and building valuations

Loan agreements and charges on assets

Lease and hire purchase agreements

All agreements signed in the last year

Product catalogues, wholesale and retail price lists

Distributor agreements

History of the Company

Date of incorporation and important events

Share Capital

Authorized and issued

Present ownership

Significant past changes

Shareholders relationships

Board

Other directorships

Interest in other companies

Relatives employed

Cars

Pensions

Loan of assets

Loan accounts

Other benefits

Consultancy agreements

Share options

Pensions to former directors

Assets

Land and Buildings

- location
- tenure
- condition
- area
- valuation
- lettings
- surplus space
- planning status
- future improvements and potential for alternative use
- insurance

Plant and Equipment

- value
- age and condition of major items
- capital expenditure — budgeted, authorized and contracted
- fixed asset register

Intellectual Property

Patents, trade marks and licence agreements

Other Assets

Investments and advances to subsidiaries and associates

Stock and work in progress

- product group analysis
- physical stock check procedures
- valuation methods and past changes
- surplus and redundant stock
- provisions
- sale or return and sample stocks

Debtors

- age analysis
- provisions
- credit terms and exceptions
- status checks
- credit collection techniques

Cash

Liabilities

Loans and Debentures

- interest rate
- conditions and terms

Creditors

- age analysis
- recording and authorization

Taxation

- corporation
- capital gains
- PAYE
- VAT
- deferred tax
- tax losses available

Overdraft

- amount
- interest rate
- limit
- review date

Profit and Loss

Sales

- product analysis
- key customer and outlet analysis
- territory analysis
- 'windfall' sales
- last and planned price increases
- discount structure and 'special' terms
- distribution channels

Products and services

- costing
- pricing

- profitability
- order book

Provisions

- movements in past and current year

Number of Employees

- by department, at beginning and end of last year and today

One-off Items

- accounting policy changes and non-recurring items in recent years

Payment to staff

- typical salaries and wages
- company cars
- overtime
- holidays
- benefits
- bonuses
- last and next reviews

Pensions

- number in scheme
- number of pensioners
- last actuarial review
- discretionary pension payments

Accounting

- accounting policies
- budgeting

- monthly reporting
- tax planning
- cash and currency management
- staff
- contingent liabilities
- profit forecasts

Advisers

Index